W9-AJU-224

The
TALIBAN
Ascent to Power

Guilderland Public Library
2228 Western Avenue
Guilderland, NY 12084-9701

The
TALIBAN
Ascent to Power

M. J. Gohari

OXFORD
UNIVERSITY PRESS

OXFORD
UNIVERSITY PRESS

Great Clarendon Street, Oxford OX2 6DP
Oxford University Press is a department of the University of Oxford.
It furthers the University's objective of excellence in research, scholarship,
and education by publishing worldwide in

Oxford New York

Athens Auckland Bangkok Bogotá Buenos Aires Cape Town Chennai
Dar es Salaam Delhi Florence Hong Kong Istanbul Karachi Kolkata
Kuala Lumpur Madrid Melbourne Mexico City Mumbai Nairobi
Paris São Paulo Shanghai Singapore Taipei Tokyo Toronto Warsaw
with associated companies in Berlin Ibadan

Oxford is a registered trade mark of Oxford University Press
in the UK and in certain other countries

© M. J. Gohari, 1999

The moral rights of the author have been asserted

First published 2000

All rights reserved. No part of this publication may be reproduced, translated,
stored in a retrieval system, or transmitted, in any form or by any means, without
the prior permission in writing of Oxford University Press.
Enquiries concerning reproduction should be sent to
Oxford University Press at the address below.

This book is sold subject to the condition that it shall not, by way
of trade or otherwise, be lent, re-sold, hired out or otherwise circulated
without the publisher's prior consent in any form of binding or cover
other than that in which it is published and without a similar condition
including this condition being imposed on the subsequent purchaser.

ISBN 0 19 579560 1

First published by Oxford Logos Society,
P. O. Box 1140, East Oxford D.O., Oxford OX4 4WP, 1999.
This edition by Oxford University Press, 2001.
Reprinted by permission Oxford Logos Society.

Fourth Impression 2002

Printed in Pakistan at
Mas Printers, Karachi.
Published by
Ameena Saiyid, Oxford University Press
5-Bangalore Town, Sharae Faisal
PO Box 13033, Karachi-75350, Pakistan.

For the children of
Afghanistan

Contents

Introduction

This book is a concise depiction of the Taliban's military, social, and political presence in Afghanistan. This is an important issue due to the fact that they—in their aspirations and understanding of Islam—echo a part of Islam that has long become a matter of heated dispute and controversy both inside the Islamic religion and outside it. Although almost all of the Western world condemned the Taliban's political agenda and military performance, and although so many Muslims indicated indignation and displeasure about so-called anti-Islamic behaviour of the Taliban, nevertheless, there were a large number of Muslims who considered the Taliban's administration as an embodiment of Islamic law and politics. The fact that the Taliban fought an Islamic government founded by the Mujahideen carries an element of irony. The Mujahideen were known world-wide for their Islamic resistance and campaign (jihad) against so-called "Soviet infidels". They represented Islam in battle, in religious and political arenas. They were praised by a wide variety of political individuals and institutions ranging from the US governments to Shi'ite mentors of the Islamic revolution in Iran. They received help and prayer and Islamic endowments simply because they were deemed by all Muslims as "the true defenders of the faith". To many Muslims, the Mujahideen represented the purest form of Islam symbolising the highest values prescribed by Allah. Mujahideen, as many Muslims believed, revived the long forgotten principle of jihad (holy war), exactly the thing that was believed to ensure the Muslims' return to their glory and magnificence. However, this view was not shared by the Taliban and their supporters. Quite ironically, they called their campaign against the Mujahideen "jihad". Claiming to be fighters of Allah, they needed to excommunicate the Mujahideen so that they could wage war against them. Perhaps the conflict within Mujahideen groups over power was the most suitable excuse that provided the Taliban with the justification they needed for their anti-Mujahideen campaign. Yet many political observers believe that the emergence of the Taliban was not merely motivated by religious incentives. They support their claim by relating the appearance of the Taliban and their rise to power with foreign interests in Afghanistan. It was staggering to many of these observers that a group of unskilled religious students whom nobody had heard of throughout the long years of jihad came out of the shadows and curbed all major Mujahideen groups in almost no time. Irrespective of all odds, the bloodshed that started with the Soviet invasion of Afghanistan still continues to ravage the lives of millions of Afghans.

In the contemporary phase of the civil war in Afghanistan, the world stands in a position of perplexity and bewilderment. Some manifestations of the Taliban rule have brought issues of mounting concern to the surface. People both in the West, and in some secularly ruled Muslim societies ask if the Taliban policies on gender, judicial system, education and individual rights are genuinely Islamic. At times the support for the Taliban expressed by Muslim hard-liners living in Western societies gives impetus to debates dealing with multiculturalism and peaceful coexistence. In areas with considerable number of the Taliban's fellow religionists such as Pakistan, the very example of the Taliban administration could put the legitimacy of the government at risk. In neighbouring countries of Afghanistan such as Iran, territorial integrity would be at stake due to centrifugal religious movements inspired and sponsored by the Taliban. The implementation of what the Taliban deem to be "Islamic law", challenges the achievements of the international community, especially on human rights and their universality. All these parameters make research about the Taliban valid and worthwhile.

This book comprises nine chapters:

The first chapter depicts Afghanistan in its historical context. Undoubtedly the texture of Afghanistan's past is of paramount significance in shaping the current events in this country. In this chapter a picture of Afghanistan in its pre-Islamic era and its Islamic history up to the Taliban rule is presented.

In the second chapter a brief introduction to main political figures of weight in jihad against the Soviets is put forward. The chapter deals with details of leading people who pioneered the campaign and formed various political parties within the Mujahideen movement. The chapter is meant to display the mentality of the Mujahideen out of whom the Taliban claim to have emerged, and against whom they run a ruthless war.

The book in its third chapter seeks to place the Taliban in a theological perspective. The Taliban are usually seen as a religious force attempting to impose their ideas and ideals by force. But what are those ideas and ideals? This is a question that falls into the heart of the Taliban's theological creed. They seem to share the main religious ethos with other major groups of the Mujahideen and yet differ from them over interpretations. The difference made by these interpretations renders the gap between the Mujahideen and the Taliban so deep that they could easily treat each other as non-Muslims. The Taliban theological platform constitutes a chief element of distinction between them and the rest of the Muslims who think or are thought to be more flexible towards modernity and its manifestations.

In the fourth chapter, I have tried to explain the political fibre of the Taliban movement. This chapter is in a way an exploration of the procedures through which the Taliban have extracted their political philosophy from Islam. Indicating the eminence of their theological basis in formation of their politics, I have also endeavoured to demonstrate the other sources of influence such as the Iranian and Saudi modules of religious political rule.

In chapter five, an original attempt is made to present an inclusive image of the Islamic economy by exploring the economic thoughts of the Taliban in a brief fashion. It has been a demanding task without which we could not possibly provide the reader with a multidimensional portrayal of an entity called the Taliban Islamic government. This chapter, at the outset, contains a host of thoughts and conceptions cultivated within the intellectual circles on the issue of the Islamic economy. Subsequently, there is a reference to the

Taliban economic agenda that could be glimpsed in the light of what occurred before their rule. Afghanistan's income-generating resources, as well as its regional and national economic criteria and activities, form another part of this chapter.

As suggested earlier, the performance of the Taliban on issues like gender and individual rights has raised serious concern internationally. To the Taliban, international individuals and institutions must bow to the will of Islam on those issues; they have simply no say in what Allah is said to have legislated for His people, and their interference would be repugnant and disrespectful to the Afghani traditions and culture. The Taliban's policies on human rights, their justifications, and their responses to international concern, are a central theme of the sixth chapter.

In chapter seven, the prospects and consequences of the interaction between the Taliban and neighbouring countries of Afghanistan are placed under the magnifying glass. All these countries, including Pakistan, Iran, Central Asian Republics, China and India, have benefits and disadvantages concerning their current and future transaction with the Taliban. These benefits and disadvantages are elaborated upon in this chapter.

Chapter eight expounds the question of Bin Laden that was and still is closely associated with the Taliban. Bin Laden's revolutionary Islam, could be seen in many ways as exemplification of the Taliban's Islam. Therefore Bin Laden's life, convictions and activities, as well as his universal views in respect of the major international powers, are identified as useful to a better understanding of Afghanistan under the Taliban.

In the ninth and conclusive chapter, I have alluded to the difficulties of the UN with the Taliban. The chapter is designed to epitomise briefly the awkwardness of Taliban's encounter with a world alien to their views and vice versa.

M. J. Gohari
Oxford
December 1999

1

Afghanistan's History

Afghanistan's historical entity is difficult to divide into clear-cut periods. In some periods its territory constituted part of larger kingdoms or empires, in others the country spread beyond its present confines, and at nearly every stage local rulers dominated semi-independent regions within a larger framework. Archaeological expeditions to Afghanistan have brought to light painted pottery of the 4th millennium BC. It has been suggested that the region north of the Hindu Kush was one of the first to be settled by people who engaged in agriculture. The survival of more than 70 varieties of wheat in the country supports this assumption. The ethnic characteristics of this aboriginal people are unknown. About 2000 BC, at the height of the Bronze Age, groups of the Indo–Aryan subdivision of the Aryans drifted south across the Oxus River. Some of these people settled in Bakhdi, the classical Bactria, while others moved to the Iranian plateau or to the Indus Basin. Their language was Indo-European, and their religion has survived in the hymns and prayers of the Rig Veda, which gives place names identifiable with the sites in Afghanistan.

Before Islam

The empire of the Achaemenids rose in southern Iran in the mid-6th century BC. It extended its control over the area north of the Hindu Kush, the Kabul Valley, and the region from Kandahar to the Indus. In the 6th century BC the Achaemenian ruler Cyrus II the Great established his authority over the area. Darius I the Great consolidated Achaemenian rule of the region through the provinces, or satrapies, of Aria (in the region of modern Herat), Bactria (Balkh), Sattagydia (Ghazni to the Indus River), Arachosia (Kandahar), and Drangiana (Seistan). Gold and silver coins of the Achaemenids have been found in Afghanistan.

Alexander the Great overthrew the Achaemenians and conquered most of the Afghan satrapies before he left for India in 327 BC. He founded the town of Alexandria Ariorum at or near the site of modern Herat. His route led through Kandahar and Ghazni and then across the Hindu Kush into Bactria. After founding a number of new towns with Greek colonists, he retraced his steps to the Kabul Valley and proceeded to the Indus. Following his death in 323, the present areas of Iran and Afghanistan fell to the Seleucid monarchy. In about 250 BC, Diodotus I, Greek satrap of the Seleucids, asserted the independence of Bactria and founded a line of 29 kings and 3 queens of the so-called Graeco-Bactrian kingdom. For a time these rulers were able to stave off invasions by tribal peoples from the north, but they could not withstand the successive waves of the Parthians, a Saka tribe, and the Yueh-chih (Yuechi). By about 140 BC the Yueh-chih had swarmed across the Oxus. While monumental remains of the Graeco-Bactrian kingdom have not been found, unmistakable Greek influence is apparent in the art of the succeeding period.

After the Yueh-chih settled in Bactria, one of its five clans, the Kushanas, gained supremacy. It produced two dynasties, the Kadphises and the Kanishkas. King Kanishka (1st or 2nd century AD), the founder and outstanding figure of his line, was a pious Buddhist responsible for codifying the principles of his religious denomination. Later Kushana rulers were subservient to the Sassanid kings of Iran, and in the 5th and 6th centuries White Huns (Ephthalites) and Turkic tribesmen moved into the area. A local dynasty, variously known as Shahiya or Ratbil, erected Buddhist monuments in the Kabul Valley in the 6th and 7th centuries.

Despite the upheavals of this period, trade flourished along the caravan route from Antioch on the Mediterranean to Bactria, Kapisa, Hadda, and Peshawar, while a northern branch of the route ran from Bactria toward China. A transplanted Buddhist culture reached a high level of spiritual and artistic achievement in Gandhara, as the region from the Kabul Valley to the Indus was then known, and the style of its monuments, painting, and sculpture is called Graeco-Buddhist Gandharan art. At Hadda, six miles south of Jalalabad, are several stupas and monasteries. Of many ancient sites near Kabul, the most notable is Kapisa, modern Bagram (Begram).

Islamic Conquest

Islamic armies defeated the Sasanians in 642 at Nahavand (near modern Hamadan, Iran) and moved on to the Afghan area, but they were unable to hold the territory; cities submitted, only to rise in revolt, and the hastily converted returned to their old beliefs once the armies had passed. The 9th and 10th centuries witnessed the rise of numerous local Islamic dynasties. One of the earliest was the Tahirids of Khorasan, whose kingdom included Balkh and Herat; they established virtual independence from the Abbasid caliphate in 820. The Tahirids were succeeded in 867-869 by a native dynasty from Seistan, the Saffarids. Local princes in the north soon became feudatories of the powerful Samanids, who ruled from Bukhara. From 872 to 999, Bukhara, Samarkand, and Balkh enjoyed a golden age under Samanid rule. Alptigin (Alptegin), a Turkish officer of the Samanids, founded the Ghaznavid dynasty in 962. Nine rulers of this line, most of them unrelated to each other, controlled a vast area from their capital in Ghazni. Mahmud, who came to the throne in 999, was the greatest of the line, conducting 17 campaigns against the Hindus and amassing vast treasures. Four hundred poets and many scientists and historians resided at Ghazni. Most of the other Ghaznavid rulers held power briefly, struggling with diminishing success against the expansion of the Seljuks, a Turkish tribe. As the power of the Ghaznavids subsided, isolated groups in the heart of the Koh-i-Baba gained strength. The heads of the Tajik Souri tribe, centred at Ghor (Ghur), established the Shansabanid dynasty at Bamiyan, while Ala-ud-Din, the leader of another branch of this line, centered at Firozkoh (Firuzkuh), captured and burned Ghazni in 1151. This Ghurid dynasty controlled Afghanistan until the early

13th century, and its rulers conducted several campaigns against India. Turkic viceroys of the Ghurids founded the sultanate at Delhi.

From the Mongol Invasion to the 19th Century

In 1219, Mongol hordes under Genghis Khan invaded the valley of the Amu Darya and then moved on to wipe out Bamiyan, Balkh, and Herat. Under a Mongol line, the Il-Khanids, who ruled in Persia from 1260 to the mid-14th century, Afghanistan was a provincial holding of little interest and importance. The indigenous Kert (Kurt) dynasty, a Tajik line related to the Ghurids, ruled at Herat as Mongol vassals during most of the 14th century. Timur (Tamerlane), another in the long line of great Asian conquerors, was born of Turko-Mongol origin in 1336 near Samarkand (Samarqand). His campaign ranged almost to. the Mediterranean on the west and into India on the east, and all of Afghanistan was under his control. On his death in 1405, his holdings were disputed by his family, and his fourth son, Shah Rukh (reigned 1405–1447), took over Afghanistan, with his capital at Herat. A cultured monarch, he made the city an intellectual centre, graced by architects, painters, poets, musicians, and scholars. His eldest son and successor, Ulugh Beg (reigned 1447–1449), was a fine painter and poet who also furthered astronomy and mathematics. Finally, at the end of the 15th century, the Timurids gave way to the Shaybanids, a Tatar dynasty. A descendant of Timur known as Babur (Baber; real name Zahir-ud-Din Muhammad Babur), after struggling vainly against his Shaybanid cousins, moved south in 1504 to take over Kabul and Kandahar. In 1525–1527 he campaigned successfully in India and established a court at Agra that was to attain great splendor under his descendants, the Mughul (Mogul) emperors. His successors, rulers such as Humayun, Akbar, and Shah Jahan, were concerned not only with India but with retaining Kabul and Kandahar against the Safavid dynasty of Persia, which finally acquired the area in the mid-17th century. In 1709 the Afghan Ghilzais revolted at Kandahar, and by 1722 they had gathered sufficient strength to move against Kerman, Yezd, and Isfahan. The Safavid ruler, Shah Husein, then abdicated in favor of the Afghan leader, Mir Mahmud ibn-Mir Wais. The Persians rallied, however, and in 1729–1730 the Afghans were driven from Persia and Herat by Nadir Kuli (reigned 1736–1747), first ruler of the Afshar dynasty, who won over the Abdalis and Ghilzais and moved east to another invasion of India. On his death in 1747 the Afghans assembled at Kandahar and chose Ahmad Khan Sadozai as their shah. So began modern united Afghanistan. Ahmad Shah was obsessed by the vision of a union of Pushtu-speaking tribes under the rule of his tribe and family, and he changed the name of his tribe from Abdali to Durrani. His reign and those of his sons and grandsons were plagued by revolts of unruly chieftains, and the kingdom of the Sadozais came to an end in the first quarter of the 19th century.

In the 19th century, Afghanistan became a focal point of international conflict. While the Kajar rulers of Persia coveted Herat, of greater moment was the concern of the British to protect the approaches to India from the advance of the Russians. To stop the Russians, Britain brought pressure to bear on Afghanistan, which resulted in two Anglo–Afghan wars (1839–1842 and 1878–1880). British policy was aimed at establishing a defensive line well beyond the Indus, and in 1839 British forces, pushing into Afghanistan, took Kandahar and Kabul and supported Shah Shuja of the Sadozai line. Internal opposition led to the withdrawal of British troops toward Peshawar in 1842. En route they were set upon by the tribes, and almost all of them were slain. Although a British punitive force reoccupied Kabul, Britain decided upon a complete evacuation of Afghanistan, thus ending the First Afghan War late that year. The British then supported Dost Mohammed (reigned 1826–1863), a Barakzai, on the Afghan throne. In 1878, British concern over negotiations between Dost Mohammed's son, Shir (Sher) Ali (reigned 1863–1878), and the Russians resulted in the Second Afghan War. This costly and futile conflict ended with the accession of Abdur Rahman Khan (reigned 1880–1901). A shrewd, forceful, and tireless ruler, he did much to diminish the power of the warlike tribes and to promote a spirit of national identity. Talks with the British in 1893 resulted in the Durand Line, which remains the boundary between Afghanistan and Pakistan. In 1901 the throne passed to Abdur Rahman's son, Habibullah Khan, during whose reign Russia and Britain concluded a treaty (1907) that recognised the buffer position of Afghanistan and the special rights of the British in respect of its foreign relations. Despite internal and external pressures, Habibullah kept his country neutral in World War I.

Development of the Modern State from Early 1900s to the Taliban Rule

Habibullah's son, Amanullah Khan (reigned 1919–1929), was resolved to bring Afghanistan abreast of the Western world. His determination that the country should be completely independent led to the brief and inconclusive Third Afghan War with Britain in 1919. By treaty, Britain then gave up its interest in Afghan foreign relations and discontinued its subsidies to the rulers. Amanullah's program of reforms included more efficient administration, the promulgation of the country's first constitution (1923), and steps taken to modernise the social structure. In 1927 he toured Europe and came back determined to work for universal education, separation of religion and state, and emancipation of women. These plans outraged religious and tribal leaders, and in an atmosphere of widespread disaffection a former brigand called Bacha-i-Saqqa was able to seize Kabul in 1929. Amanullah abdicated and fled the country.

The brigand ascended the throne as Amir Habibullah, but powerful forces led by four brothers of the Mohammedzai family soon rose against him. One of the brothers took Kabul in October and was acclaimed as the new ruler, Nadir Shah Ghazi. Order was re-established, a constitution was passed, and a series of sound measures undertaken, but an internal feud resulted in Nadir Shah's assassination in 1933.

His eldest son, Mohammed Zahir Shah, then 19, was proclaimed king, but in the following decades his uncles directed the destiny of the country, holding the major cabinet posts. Two first cousins of the ruler, Mohammed Daud and Mohammed Naim, were also cabinet members. During these years the government abandoned the traditional policy of isolation, and the first factories, motor roads, and irrigation and power projects were constructed. In World War II, Afghanistan maintained its neutrality, but inability to trade with foreign countries resulted in a strain on its finances. Mohammed Daud became premier in 1953, and for a decade government policy was directed by a triumvirate consisting of Mohammed Zahir Shah, Mohammed Daud, and Mohammed Naim as minister of foreign affairs.

In the late 1950s the Shah began to institute social and political reforms and to broaden the base of authority of his government. In 1963 Premier Mohammed Daud resigned and the cabinet was replaced by one headed by Premier Mohammed Yusuf, the first non-royal premier. Meanwhile, a new constitution was adopted in 1964; members of the royal family could no longer participate in politics, although the king retained substantial power. The legislature and executive were often at loggerheads, and the government functioned inefficiently.

On July 17, 1973, the king's cousin and former premier, Mohammed Daud, overthrew the monarchy with the help of the Soviet-trained Afghan Army and was named president and premier of the new republic. The abrogated 1964 constitution was replaced with another in 1977, which confirmed the presidential form of government in a one-party state. However, Daud's hold over the army that had backed his bid for power in 1973, weakened during 1977, and in April 1978 his government was overthrown in a military revolt and he was killed.

This "Great Saur Revolution" (April 27–28, 1978) led to the establishment of the Democratic Republic of Afghanistan (the 1977 constitution was annulled), with the People's Democratic Party of Afghanistan (PDPA) the only legitimate party; its leader, Nur Mohammed Taraki, became president of the council and premier. The Soviet Union extended its support, and the two countries signed a Treaty of Friendship in December 1978.

The newly established Marxist state was not popular with the Muslim tribal communities, and they revolted. To quell the rebellion, the Soviet Union provided arms and military advisers. There was also serious infighting in the PDPA, however, and in September 1979, Taraki was ousted from office and replaced by the premier, Hafizullah Amin. When Amin could not end the rebellion, the Soviet Union intervened and invaded Afghanistan with 30,000 troops in late December. Amin was executed, and the Soviets installed Babrak Karmal as president on December 27, 1979. Afghan resistance to the Soviet intervention was widespread; it was met with the introduction of more Soviet troops, eventually numbering an estimated 115,000. In the face of the fighting, a flood of Afghan refugees sought sanctuary in Pakistan and Iran.

The rebel guerrillas, known as the Mujahideen ("holy warriors"), were far from united. Guerrilla bands often represented fiercely independent tribes with long histories of mutual antagonism. Their main strength was in the countryside, while Afghan government forces and their Soviet allies concentrated on the larger towns and cities. Arms supplied mostly by the United States and China were funnelled to the guerrillas through Pakistan, where their political leaders were based. Over time the power of the field commanders inside Afghanistan grew at the expense of that of their political leaders, tending to complicate the lines of guerrilla leadership still further. From the end of 1986, when a real Soviet desire to withdraw its troops became evident, the question of whether the guerrilla movement could provide a representative leadership capable of governing Afghanistan became increasingly acute.

For its part, while conducting the war, Karmal's elite Parcham (Flag) faction of the PDPA struggled for control with its Khalq (Masses) faction, which had dominated it before the Saur revolution. Various measures were taken to ensure the Parcham's grip on the party, including, in 1985, the introduction of a new constitution. But in May 1986, Karmal was out-manoeuvred not by the Khalq but by fellow Parcham member Major General Najibullah, who became general secretary of the PDPA and later Afghanistan's president, gradually relieving Karmal of his posts. Attempts by Najibullah, the former head of the secret police, to draw the Mujahideen into his "national reconciliation" failed. Another constitution, adopted in 1987, greatly increased Najibullah's power and renamed the country the Republic of Afghanistan. A UN-brokered agreement for Soviet withdrawal was reached in April 1988; the withdrawal was completed in February 1989. But the flow of arms to both sides and the continued divisions among the rebels kept the bloody civil war alive.

Najibullah remained in power until April 1992, when the Mujahideen captured Kabul and proclaimed it an Islamic state. The Mujahideen ruled the nation through several councils, including the Resolution and Settlement Council, which on December 30, 1992, elected the Islamic State of Afghanistan's first president, Burhanuddin Rabbani. The Mujahideen remained factionalised, however, and sporadic fighting continued. In March 1993 a peace accord was signed by Rabbani, his chief rival Gulbuddin Hekmatyar, and other Mujahideen factions. An 18-month interim government was established, with Rabbani as head of state and Hekmatyar as premier, but they proved unable to work together. By the end of 1994 the peace accord had collapsed, and the fighting between rival Mujahideen forces escalated. At the same time another militant group, the Taliban, arose in southern Afghanistan, capturing the cities of Qandahar and Charasiab, former strongholds of Hekmatyar's forces. Defeated in their mid-1995 assault against Kabul, the Taliban continued their bombardments of the city, eventually taking it on September 27, 1996, and establishing a new government for Afghanistan based on Islamic law.

2

The Mujahideen

The word Mujahideen is derived from jihad, a Quranic term denoting the battle against Allah's enemies. It is narrated that jihad falls theologically into two categories, jihad with one's carnal ego, and also fight against human adversaries. Apparently the first kind of jihad is preferred over the second one. The first holy war to be announced against other Muslims occurred when a group of the slain Caliph Osman sought revenge on Muslim conspirators. Since then the Islamic world has witnessed bloody struggles between various Muslim factions who frequently called their strife for dominance "jihad". All groups apparently desired to have Allah on their side. This was ideal due to providing both religious legitimacy and loyalty of life-sacrificing soldiers. The scale of inter-Islamic wars is incomparably large. Perhaps the bloodiest conflict that ever happened within the Islamic society was the Iran-Iraq war which lasted for more than eight consecutive years and caused some 1000,000 dead and a larger number of disabled and dislocated persons and families. The concept and indentity of Islamic internal wars have always been a matter of deep political and theological disagreement. Even in the 1990 Gulf War which resulted in occupation of Kuwait by Iraq, there remained some Muslim countries and groups such as the Jordanians and Palestinians who indicated reluctance to support the liberation efforts by the rest of the Islamic world. However, these Muslim groups were more prepared to grant their support to wars in which "believers" directly confronted "disbelievers". In modern times the Soviet invasion of Afghanistan was a common ground of agreement within the Islamic sphere. The range of those who backed "jihad" in Afghanistan was wide and brought the political attitudes of people like Ayatollah Khomeini of Iran closer to those of King Fahad and King Hussayn in the Arab world.

Mujahideen movement in reaction to the Russian invasion was preceded with a cultural Islamic revivalism in the Islamic world that had started a new phase in the seventies. The rise of Islamic intellectual movement itself was a natural response to challenges levelled by materialistic Marxism to traditional Islam in Afghanistan. Assuming that Marxism and secularism in general place Islamic traditional values and principles in jeopardy, a number of Muslim intellectuals sought to find solutions which were in conformity with the spirit of modernity and simultaneously approved by Islam. This understanding was backed by the Islamic success of previously shaped intellectual movements. For example, the Muslim Brotherhood in Egypt has always been a source of inspiration to other Muslim revivalists across the Islamic world including Shi'ite Iranians. The political modifications of theology by Mawdudi in Pakistan also provided the ground for forward-looking Muslims elsewhere to take methods of mass mobilisation of Muslims inaugurated by him and his successors into consideration. Emergence of the Taliban and their claim to unique representation of Islam, opened a new arena of investigation on Islam and its true face as seen differently by various beholders.

Evidently the Mujahideen groups were mainly and still are influenced by the personality of their founders. Irrespective of groups such as Hizb-i-Wahdat whose ideological link with Iran makes the impact of its leader a secondary issue, the major parties embody the philosophical and administrative views of founder members. That is the reason why a glimpse of biographical details of these leaders can be of significance to a better understanding of the jihad and its related later events.

Burhanuddin Rabbani

Rabbani was born in 1940 in Badakhshan. After completion of school education in his native province, he enrolled in *Darul-uloom-e-Sharia* (Abu Hanifa), a well-known religious school in Kabul.

When he graduated from Abu-Hanifa, he went to Kabul University to study Islamic Law and Theology. Soon after his graduation in 1963, he was employed by Kabul University in a teaching capacity. To further his education, he travelled to Egypt in 1966 where he came in close contact with the infrastructure of the Islamic movement there. In Egypt, he had the opportunity of meticulously scrutinising the political awakening of the Muslim intelligentsia as well as getting familiar with some of the leading figures. His studies at Al-Azhar installed the embryonic part of liberal theology of Islam in his mind.

In 1968, Rabbani returned to Afghanistan, where the High Council of Jamiat-i-Islami of Afghanistan commissioned him to supervise the Jamiat's students branch.

In 1972, he was selected to lead the Jamiat-i-Islami of Afghanistan. In the spring of 1974, with the rise of political suppression he was wanted for his political opposition to Afghan authorities. He managed to escape to the countryside.

In short Rabbani might be considered as a Muslim scholar with the experience of cosmopolitan societies of the Islamic world. Since he received some education in Egypt, he must have encountered the Islamic schools of thought founded by people such as Mohammad Abuh, Rashid Reza, Hasan al-Banna, Sayyed Qutb, and other Egyptian reformists who sought to exalt the word of Islam through modern interpretation of the old tradition. A fluent speaker of Persian, Rabbani was supposed to have known the renowned Muslim reformists in Iran who pursued the very same ideas of their Egyptian counterparts but via their own approaches, scholars like Dr Ali Shari'ati, Mahdi Bazargan and others.

His approaches to issues of concern Islamically as the head of government shows a resemblance to methods used by so-called Liberal minded leaders of Iranian revolution, individuals such as Mahdi Bazargan, the prime minister of interim government and Bani Sadr, the first president of the Iranian revolution. What makes this comparison of interest is the fact that both Bazargan and Banisadr were removed from their posts being accused of not representing "true Islam". In the context of present study it is of significance to pay attention to some of the main characteristics of Rabbani's movement.

The party led by Rabbani was founded by Niazi, a Muslim intellectual who was killed in the seventies. Jamiat-e-Islami believes that the highest historical prides and honours of Afghan society are related to those periods when Islamic culture prevailed in all aspects of the nation. The party concentrates on enormous historical contributions of Afghan society to culture and civilisation which were only made possible through domination of Islam. Rabanni's party has frequently made it clear that accomplishments such as creation of strong unity among different tribes and races, establishment of powerful central governments, effective participation of Afghan people in the world's intellectual life, breaking the chains of imperialism for the first time in the East, and tens of other examples, are all due to teachings and instructions of Islam.

Jamiat holds that there is an imperialistic conspiracy against Afghanistan as a result of severe defeats inflicted on so-called colonialism by Afghan nation in a unique fashion. They constantly repeat that "after the year 1919 when Afghans raised the flag of jihad in the light of Islamic jihad and inflicted incurable injuries to the strongest colonial country of the world, the initiation of such a revolution from this small nation placed it ahead of all heroic nations of the world and made all imperial castles to shake. Because of these heroic activities the wicked imperialist networks reacted severely against the revolutionary initiatives of our people with new methods. They spared no efforts to remove the eternal teachings of Islam from peoples life. Agents of imperialism, with the help of oppressive governments, prevented the implementation of Islamic principles and instead, tried to play tricks with the people by their pretence to Islam."

Jamiat-e-Islami's official mission is:
- To protect Islamic teachings
- To defend deprived classes
- To retain of national prestige
- To represent Afghanistan Muslim peoples desires

The party prides itself for having a longer history of struggle than others. As a matter of fact within the complicated structure of political rivalry in contemporary Afghanistan, the party considers its veteran campaign as irrefutable evidence of legitimacy. This is often used against individuals and parties contending or challenging the Jamiat over territorial acquisition or ideological maxims. The following words denoting a wide range of the Jamiat's adversaries is in common use; "During the rule of the King, it was only the revolutionary voice of Jamiat's faithful members that shook the severely corrupted government organisations and like a violent storm took away both rest and peace from the criminals and evildoers. Similarly, when our weak nation was brutally tortured during Daud's cruel regime, when the political and economic independence fell into danger, and when our history and culture were going to destruction, it was only the loud cry of Jamiat affiliates which was heard and no cry from the others at all. These false revolutionaries of today bowed their heads down before the wicked powers in those times. They were committing crimes such as looting people's wealth and property, killing and slaughtering the Afghan youth. It was only Jamiat-e-Islami Afghanistan that continued its wide revolutionary struggle under difficult situations and spared no attempts in making sacrifices. It was the brave Mujahideen of this organisation who tolerated the inhuman tortures and hardship of dark cells of the prisons to protect Islamic principles and to make free their tortured nation. After the bloody coup of 7th of Saur, the situation changed and our dear country was falling into the mouth of the social Imperialist dragon. Inferior slaves and country-selling elements have changed this country into a horrible prison. Nothing is heard in this prison but the noise of creaking racks and crying of tortured prisoners."

On social reforms it is again Jamiat's mode to employ Islamic terms with implications which might be somewhat different from what is literally understood by them. *Jaheliat*, an Islamic term, which technically denotes everything against the illumination of the Islamic revelation is used in the Party's literature to indicate the appalling state of economy. This is indeed an innovative interpretation of the quoted term which contains the preliminary element of a modernist understanding of Islam. The Party's statements insist that it wants to eliminate poverty, deprivation, unemployment, oppression, colonialism, injustice and all "shameful results of *Jaheliat*" (ignorance) systems.

A series of social and economic reforms are proposed by the Jamiat. They say that they want to bring about such conditions in which the basic needs of the people are met and they live in peace and prosperity; conditions in which people's dignity is safeguarded and their rights are not violated, and conditions in which people's wealth and properties are safe from looting and arson. They have proclaimed that they intend to distribute uncultivated lands amongst the landless farmers and those who have little land for cultivation, and to raise workers' living standards.

At national level Jamiat's announced attitudes represent a strong struggle against unfair privileges, linguistic and regional prejudices and hostile factionalism, bringing unity among all races and tribes as well as to provide better opportunity for equal rights and obligations, equal participation of all Afghans in developing their country. Jamiat considers protection of minorities as its Islamic obligation.

On gender issue, Jamiat announces that it wants the women to be able to utilise those rights and privileges given to them by Islamic eternal teachings. Jamiat also wants all women to get their proper status in the pure Islamic society. This, however, requires more clarification as to what in Jamiat's view the women's proper status would be.

Internationally, the official policies of Jamiat are as follows:

- It supports all freedom loving movements whose policies are based on defending the rights of the oppressed.
- It wants good relations with all nations of the world.
- It firmly support unity and solidarity among Muslim countries.
- It backs strengthening the non-aligned movements against aggressive and colonial powers.
- Jamiat considers it a duty to provoke the spirit of jihad in all brave Afghan Muslims in order to assure the progress and

strengthening of the world wide Islamic call, to break the chain of tyranny and oppression, and to wipe out all criminal enemies of Islam.

Along with Rabbani's Jamiat is the party of another chief player in Afghanistan who must be considered the only hindrance faced by the Taliban to achieve complete domination, namely Ahmad Shah Masoud.

Ahmad Shah Masoud

Ahmad Shah Masoud used to be the vice-president and defence minister of the Islamic Government of Afghanistan under President Rabbani. However he is the last major surviving force of groups known as Mujahideen. Masoud was born in the year 1953 in the village of Jangalak, Bazarak district of Panjshir valley.

He was born to a family that had immigrated from "Par-e-Darya", today's Tajikistan, to Afghanistan. The name of this family was "Nawroozkhel". Masoud received his primary and secondary education in Lesa-e-Isteqlal. Later Ahmad Shah Masoud joined Kabul Polytechnic.

During the reign of Daud Khan, he along with other members of a party called "Jawanan-e-Musulman" (the Muslim Youth) fled to Pakistan. Jawanan-e-Musulman had been founded by Abdul Raheem Niazai. It is not quite clear when Masoud joined the Jawanan group. It appears that at the time he fled to Pakistan he was not a distinguished member of the movement.

Later and as a result of severe political controversies Ahmad decided that his political aspiration was more likely to be fulfilled through another party. To him this party must pursue a set of objectives which represent Islamic originality and contemporary realities at the same time. Masoud withdrew from Jawanan and joined Rabbani's newly created party in Pakistan. Seemingly Jawanan which had adopted radical approaches to seeking power was unable to meet this as a result of prevalent socio-political circumstances at the time. It is reported that failure of the group in a *coup* attempt caused a deep rift in leadership. Masoud, having politically a strong sense of direction soon found out that this category of radicalism was not to succeed due to lack of public support.

The Jawanan movement was resurrected when in April 1978 the communists took over Kabul. It gained more importance when in December 1979 the Soviet army invaded Afghanistan. This was a time when the need for Islamic military action, as promoted by Jawanan, was felt more than ever. During this period the people rose against the Communist regime and the invading force. This uprisal gave the Jawanan an opportunity to return to Afghanistan. Masoud, who by now had been appointed a Jamiat commander in Panjshir, returned to Panjshir in the winter of 1979-80.

He was the first person to equip Panjshir combatants with ammunition needed to confront the Communists. In spring of 1980 he began his first battle against the government and the Soviets. Within a period between 1980 to 1981, Masoud liberated most of the Panjshir valley from the control of Communist elements and undertook some major battles in the region. This made him one of the important commanders in the area and attracted both the attention of Kabul regime as well as Western journalists. Masoud's ability to speak some French brought him a good deal of publicity. By the end of 1981 he had succeeded in bringing back security to areas under his control.

Between 1982 and 1984, Masoud laid the foundation of an assembly called Shura-e-Nazar. This assembly was meant to bring legitimacy to his governance and was ultimately supervised by himself. The establishment of this kind of assembly is a predominant dimension of Afghan political and tribal history. The concept of Shura as an assembly for consultation and decision making is originally recommended by the Quran itself; however, like so many other issues it has been a subject of various interpretations.

Masoud's capability for applying all military contingencies is a well-known fact. It is reported that he was constantly being aided with intelligence flowing to him through Western organisations. He could acquire not only information on the government but also strategic data on other Mujahideen's activities. Perhaps, this kind of intelligence awareness was and still is the source of his well-organised military and political attitudes and coalitions. It is rumoured that his network of spies represents a drastic discrepancy between him and his opponents in both quantity and quality of the intelligence he receives from all sides of the conflict. It is noteworthy that his excellent communication skills, together with his military stands, have enabled him to establish meaningful contacts with major sources of both intelligence and weaponry.

It seems that with regard to all ingredients of success in Masoud's record, one has to observe his ethnic origin as a Persian Tajik, as an element that stands between him and his ultimate political ambition. Perhaps, this element played a decisive role in convincing his supporters that not being a Pashtun he may not be able to create the necessary tribal alliances and consequently fail to achieve the stability and a long-lasting and desperately required cease-fire.

Gulbuddin Hekmatyar

Gulbuddin Hekmatyar has played an important part in shaping the recent history of Afghanistan. Originally from Baghlan, he is the head and founder of Hizb-i-Islami. Hekmatyar first studied at the military academy, then in 1968, he switched to the engineering department of Kabul University. It is said that although Hekmatyar is sometimes referred to as Engineer Hekmatyar, he never graduated from Kabul University with a degree in engineering. He is frequently described as the most outspoken leader of all Afghan politicians. It is predominantly believed that Hekmatyar, before adopting an Islamic approach to politics spent four years in the PDPA (People's Democratic Party of Afghanistan). The PDPA was the Afghan communist party comprising both Parchami and Khalqi groups. Hizb members and Hekmatyar refute stories relating him to this Communist background, and consider it an insult. In 1972, Hekmatyar was put in prison for alleged killing of a Maoist student. He then fled to Pakistan and founded Hizb-i-Islami. It is widely rumoured that in 1975, Hekmatyar instigated the anti-Daoud insurrection in Panjshir.

Among accusations levelled against Hekmatyar was the accusation by almost every other political party of him being a puppet of Pakistan and the United States. The fact is that although he was in receipt of enormous foreign aid, he was always fully aware of his own interests. It is also strongly believed he had close connections with the ISI (secret service) of Pakistan, and that he was extensively trained by them. Hekmatyar's approach to power particularly in the aftermath of Mujahideen's formation of government are sharply criticized. In fact, many Afghan political analysts accuse Hekmatyar of killing more Mujahideen members than Communists. When the Communist regime fell in Kabul, Hekmatyar and his party were invited by the new Mujahideen government to take part and help build an Islamic government in Afghanistan. Hekmatyar was offered the Prime Minister's position, but he declined. He accused the Mujahideen government as un-Islamic, and in contrast with people's will. As most political analysts predicted, Hekmatyar emerged as one of the most formidable enemies of the Islamic government, created by Mujahideen leaders such as Burhanuddin Rabbani. Hekmatyar refused to discuss power sharing with other political parties and launched several unsuccessful efforts to seize power by force in Kabul.

Hekmatyar's rocket attacks created tremendous hardships for the ordinary people of Kabul, and inflicted heavy material losses to the government and people. It is held by commentators on Afghan affairs that because of Hekmatyar's military action against the Islamic government of Afghanistan, the government was weakened so much that the Taliban militia had a tremendous advantage when they started their campaign against the government. By the end of the 1992, he reached a deal with General Dostum and Hizb-i-Wahdat to form a common front against the government. Dostum and Hizb-i-Wahdat were Hekmatyar's former enemies. Rocket attacks on Kabul degraded Hekmatyar in the eyes of the ordinary Afghan.

In the beginning of 1993, Hekmatyar was again offered the seat of Prime Minister, and this time he accepted. He served as Prime Minister from March 1993, until January 1994. In early 1994, Hekmatyar, not satisfied with his power with the government aligned himself once again with Dostum to topple Rabbani's Islamic

government; they failed. Nevertheless, the Mujahideen government tried again to reach a peaceful settlement with Hekmatyar. His rocket attacks had almost completely destroyed Kabul, and the government lost much power holding back Hekmatyar's attack. In June of 1996, Hekmatyar once again accepted the position of Prime Minister.

In late 1996, the Taliban overran Kabul and forced Rabbani and Hekmatyar to flee north.

Younus Khalis

Perhaps the political movement led by Younus Khalis is not as significant as other parties in terms of political domination and previous military achievement, but with regards to its impact on the Taliban movement it must be studied as the launching platform of the Taliban. Mulla Mohammad Umar, the leader of Taliban is reported to have been an aide to Khalis's leadership in jihad against Soviet invasion of Afghanistan. This must be added to the fact that Hizb-i-Islami of Khalis has always been characterised by a type of Islamic extremism which is quite unique in comparison to other parties.

Khalis, now in his late seventies, is a graduate of traditional circles of Islamic learning with the title of Mawlavi. Mawlavi is a title usually granted to those known as professional scholars of Islamic heritage. However it must be mentioned that on occasions these scholars have taken up professions other than preaching to the public or teaching in schools or research on theology and law. Before the rise of political Islam in non-Arab parts of the Middle East, the *Ulema* (Muslim scholars) were present in politics purely on a voluntary basis. However with the formation of government in Iran, they occupied positions with guaranteed salaries and frequent bonuses. In an overall view, one can observe nowadays an increasing number of these scholars who no longer concern themselves with issues which previously obsessed them such as achieving academic excellence, rather they are engaged in partisan politics leading to civil or military conflicts or ultimately to high governmental ranks.

Younus Khalis is an eminent member of the Pashtun community as well. He is said to have achieved enormous popularity through his strict form of Islam and personal charisma resulting from qualities such as poetry.

Khalis laid the foundation of Hizb-i-Islami which was considered a product of the split between him and Hekmatyar in the seventies. Khalis's personalty is significant by the fact that the Taliban leader, currently called *Amirul mu'minin* (Commander of the faithful) fought and lost one eye under his political and spiritual leadership. Mulla Umar, now in his thirties, must have been quite young performing jihad under Khalis. The implicit implication could be a better understanding of the formative period of Umar in Hizb-i-Islami and the size and quality of Khalis's influence as a master of religion and war on young Umar, and as a result in Afghanistan today. The proclamation of support and allegiance made by Khalis for the Taliban is supporting indication of his role.

Abd al-Rab Rasul Sayyaf

Sayyaf is another example of Islamic revolutionary graduates of Kabul University, Department of Islamic Studies. It seems that a modern academic institution played a decisive role in creating a new kind of confidence in this generation's intellectual struggle with ideological maxims and principles of Marxism and Communism. Perhaps the reluctance of traditional scholars at the secular modernisation of the country was not methodologically vigorous enough to face challenges posed by scientific Marxism and the new generation of Muslim theologians graduating from Kabul University felt that being equipped with new scientific approaches, they could now effectively stand the challenge.

Sayyaf is the leader of Ittehad-i-Islami (Islamic Unity). In his early days he developed an awareness of conflict as the main cause of failure amongst the global Muslim community in general and in Afghanistan in particular. His later association and alliance with Rabbani is a demonstration of this conception. None the less, the ups and downs of a long civil war and temporary and evanescent alliances between former enemies gave rise to doubts as to whether or not these alliances were genuinely designed to serve the greater Islamic cause or intended to secure temporal ends. What makes fair judgement virtually impossible is the huge gap of information on circumstantial movements of various factions in the midst of a fully-fledged civil war. The tiny islands of truth are surrounded by awesome oceans of myths and rumours. As far as Sayyaf is concerned he has always been the centre of rumours suggesting that he was the most favourite Mujahideen leader of Saudi Arabia. The rumours link him to Saudi government simply because of his excellent command of the Arabic language. For those who still have a recollection of Mujahideen's publicly known connections and trips to Saudi Arabia, Pakistan and even the United States, the aid received by Afghan Islamic parties is not an enigma. However the size of these groups dependability to these powers in terms of aid, intelligence, finance, remain an issue for the future to explore. No doubt, Sayyaf's linguistic gifts made him a more presentable leader of Mujahideen, however it would be naive to believe the extent of aid received by him was far larger.

Sayyaf's achievement may not measure up to those of other commanders such as Shah Masoud, but his history of jihad dating back to Zahir Shah's time gives him the credit of pioneering the Islamic movement.

Sayyed Ahmad Gailani

Jihad is just an added value to his unparalleled high status as hereditary head of the Qaderiyya Sufi fraternity. He is by birth a descendant of Shaykh Abdul Qadir Gailani, one of the most influential masters of the Middle Ages Sufis whose impact is strongly felt throughout the Islamic world. He succeeded to his position upon the death of his older brother, Sayyed Ali, in 1964. Born in 1932 and a son of Sayyed Hasan Gailani, he was educated at Abu Hanifa College. He left Afghanistan after the Saur Revolution and founded the National Islamic Front (NIFA) in Peshawar. His party is part of the seven-member coalition which in 1989 formed the "Afghan Interim Government". Although he is reported to have declined posts in the interim government for some time, he later accepted the post of supreme justice. He is frequently described as the most Western-oriented of all Afghan Mujahideen leaders.

Nabi Mohammadi

He is another Pashtun leader whose group was considered to be one of the largest among Mujahideen parties in the early eighties. His party called Harkati-Inqilabi-Islami was one of the best organised in the early periods of jihad. This might be due to a number of facts. Born in 1921, he was in his fifties when the Islamic movement rose in the seventies. In the 1950, he was one of the first members of the religious establishment who agitated against leftist movement in the country. He was elected to the parliament in 1964 and became an MP. In 1978, after the Saur Revolution, he fled to Pakistan and utilised a network of mawlavis to organise armed resistance against Kabul regime. His Pashtun origin as well as his long-standing career as a seasoned member of the Islamic movement qualified him to form one of the most successful jihad groups with the start of war. However reasons such as indecision of the Afghan situation caused his party to lose ground gradually.

Ayatollah Mazari

Although killed in 1994, Mazari must be remembered as the main Shi'ite figure in the jihad era. In 1979, with the rise of political Islam Ayatollah Khomeni criticized the Soviet Union for invasion of "Islamic" Afghanistan. To him Afghanistan was no longer a cause of united Persian front. He had implicitly declared his opposition to Persian nationalism in favour of an Islamic internationalism. However internal turmoil resulted by opposition militants in Kurdistan and elsewhere together with the start of a merciless war with Iraq diverted the attention of Iran's new statesmen to issues of higher priority. The understanding of Iranian officials at the time was mostly a result of reports they received from new Afghan Shi'ite friends and media. For a good number of years after 1979 there was no such thing as intelligence services to monitor and register the details of events in Afghanistan. This coincided with carefully premeditated plans of Pakistani government which followed and even shaped the events with consistency from the monarchy era. Having accommodated some two million Afghan refugees, Iranians were keen to play a more important role in Afghanistan and became extremely displeased to find themselves being constantly excluded in regional and global talks aiming at ending the war. They realised that they could not exercise influence unless they were represented by one or a number of conflicting factions of some strength. Mazari's role in formation of a new front to represent Shi'ism and Iran must be looked at in this context.

Mazari was born in 1935 in a Shi'ite family and received primary religious education in Afghanistan. Then determined to become an outstanding scholar he took the trouble of travelling to Najaf, an Iraqi town which is famous for its 1000 years old school of Shi'ite learning. Since this was the main site of Shi'ite scholarship before Iran-Iraq war and a place where a large number of current Iranian theocrats sought their religious education, it would be no surprise if Mazari had made the acquaintance of a considerable number of these. He even shared the title "ayatollah" usually applied to the Iranian clergymen of some high rank. In 1980, he was elected chairman of the "Afghan Shi'ia Alliance", supported by the Iran Government and headquartered in Iran during the jihad; but later it moved to Quetta (Pakistan). In June 1990, the shi'ite groups announced formation of a new organisation, called "Hizb-i-Wahadat" (Unity Party). One of its known allies was Mazari who led the alliance after the Mujahideen attained power. Ali Mazari was killed in a conspiracy by Pashtun Mujahideen groups in 1994. The alliance involved in many bloody clashes with Mujahideen Pashtun groups, particularly with Hizb-i-Islami of Gulbuddin Hekmatyar.

Mazari is granted the exalted status of "martyr" by Iranians. However there are still Shi'ite Afghans and Iranians who blame him for misleading Iranian officials and also associating himself and the

Shi'ite cause with unreliable allies thereby jeopardising the whole Shi'ite population. Following Mazari's death he was succeeded by Karim Khalili who maintains strong links with Iran. It must be borne in mind that not all Shi'ite political activists support Iran. The horizon of ideas and attitudes of the Shi'ites towards the current government in Iran is largely broad. There are Shi'ites who believe that the Iranian government based on domination of clergy is democratically unrepresentative and there are Shi'ites who think that by adopting democratic values such as elected institutions, the Iranian government has been disloyal to political ideal of Islam.

3

The Taliban's Islamic Theology

The Taliban movement represents first of all a new demonstration of the Islamic faith. Although the leaders of this movement have sought political power through military action, it seems that public opinion world-wide is more obsessed with the Islamic color of their activity rather than their military tactics and political strategy. This is mostly due to the fact that in a country where various factions fight and kill their fellow countrymen the Taliban needed reasons better than sheer longing for power to physically eliminate forces known previously as Muslim crusaders fighting for Allah. Indeed, they needed a supreme religious legitimacy which would enable them to justify shedding forbidden blood of fellow Muslims and toppling an Islamic government formed on the relentless efforts of eighteen years of jihad against the heathen Communists in the name of Islam. Only Islam itself was and is capable of granting such a legitimacy.

The Taliban perpetually announced that they were fighting merely for the word of Islam to remain transcendent. However, at the same time they emphasised that their first task was to purify the country from the stains of hypocrisy that manifested themselves in the so-called Mujahideen. Mujahideen internal conflicts, which inflicted heavy damages and huge suffering on Afghanistan, provided the Taliban with a golden chance to verify their claim over the corruption and hypocrisy of their opponents.

The broadly publicised attachment of the Taliban to a category of Islam that is palpably dissimilar to other kinds of Islam previously known to the area, such as Iranian Islam, raises questions on the nature of the theology adopted by the Taliban. It must be said at the outset of this succinct exploration of the Taliban Islam that their

Islam is certainly not at odds with other kinds of Islam represented by other Muslims and it is just the manifestation of this Islam in a special time and place which makes it distinguishable. It is indeed so with the Hanafite school of Islam which is being overwhelmingly adhered to among the Muslims of India, Pakistan and Afghanistan. This is the same school that the Taliban themselves are descended from. The methodological approach of the Taliban to this school is a matter of political as well as academic concern.

The Hanafite School

The Hanafite school or Hanafyyah is also called *Madhhab Hanafi* in Islam and is one of the four main Sunni schools of religious law, incorporating the legal opinions of the ancient Iraqi schools of Al-Kufah and Basra. The Hanafite legal system developed from the teachings of the theologian and jurisprudent Imam Abu Hanifah (c. 700–767) by such disciples as Abu Yusuf (d.798) and became the official system of Islamic legal interpretation for the Abbasids, Seljuqs, and Ottomans. In spite of the fact that the Hanafites acknowledge the Quran and Hadith (narratives concerning the Prophet's life and sayings) as primary sources of law, they are noted for the acceptance of personal opinion (*ra'y*) in the absence of precedent. Presently the school predominates in Central Asia, India, Pakistan, Turkey, and the countries of the former Ottoman Empire.

In the course of Islamic studies, the life and thoughts of Abu Hanifah, the originator of the Hanafite school, occupy a very special position. The founder of the school, was a noted Muslim jurist, jurisprudent and theologian whose systemisation of Islamic legal doctrine was so widely acknowledged that it became one of the four canonical schools of law in Sunnite Islam. He received his education in Kufah, an intellectual center of Iraq, and belonged to the Mawlavi, the non-Arab Muslims who pioneered intellectual activity in Islamic lands. The ancestors of Imam-al-Azam (the Greatest Imam as called by his followers) came from Persia, or Iran. His father, Thabit, had reportedly met Imam 'Ali (the first Imam of Shi'ite Muslims) in Kufa, and Imam 'Ali had pronounced a benediction over him and his descendants. Abu Hanifah is also considered to be one of the most eminent members of the Tabe'in (the second generation of early Muslims) and is said to have met Anas ibn Malik and a number of other immediate disciples of the Prophet.

In early youth Abu Hanifah was attracted to theological debates but later, disenchanted with theology, he turned to law and for about 18 years was a disciple of Eammad (d.738), then the most noted Iraqi jurist. After Eammad's death, Abu Hanifah became his successor. He also learned from several other scholars, notably the founder of the Shi'ite school of Islam, Ja'far-al-Sadiq, who instituted the fundamental doctrines of Shi'ite theology. Abu Hanifah's mind was also matured by extensive travels and by exposure to the heterogeneous, advanced society of Iraq. The significance of his works rests in the fact that through them he incorporated a bulk of solutions which were later applied effectively and reliably. By Abu Hanifah's time a vast body of legal doctrines had accumulated as a result of the endeavour to apply Islamic norms to legal problems. The disagreements in these doctrines had rendered necessary the development of a uniform code. He responded by scrutinising the current doctrines in collaboration with his students, several of them outstanding scholars, and had each legal problem discussed before formulating any doctrines. Before Abu Hanifah's time, doctrines had been formulated mainly in response to actual problems, whereas he attempted to solve problems that might arise in the future. By the introduction of this method, the area of law was considerably enlarged. Because of this enlargement of the bounds of law and because of Abu Hanifah's somewhat rationalist orientation and his reserve about traditions that were not highly authenticated, his school was sometimes erroneously denounced as the school of *ra'y* (independent opinion) as opposed to that of *Hadith* (authoritative tradition). Although theology was not Abu Hanifah's primary concern, he did take distinct positions on several theological questions, stimulating the development of the Maturidiyyah school, a champion of orthodoxy. Because of his temperament and academic preoccupation, he took no direct part in court politics or power struggles, despite his obvious antipathy toward the Umayyads and Abbasids, the ruling dynasties of the time. His sympathies lay with the Alids (Ali and his descendants, later revered by Shi'ites), whose revolts he openly supported with words and money. This fact partly explains why Abu Hanifah steadfastly refused a judgeship and also why he suffered severe persecution under both dynasties.

Three main points in the Hanafite school and Abu Hanifah's life are of particular interest to the study of contemporary Hanafites in general and the Taliban in particular.

1. Abu Hanifah's school of religious thought is chiefly characterised by some kind of breakaway from current traditions and a tendency towards the application of human intellect in clarification and interpretation of the revelation. This is highly significant in the view that Hanafites are equipped with appropriate tools as well as sufficient liberty to bring together the long-standing traditions of Islam with the requirements of modern life. Questions such as the exorbitant attachment to old styles of Islamic life which usually arise in some Islamic schools such as the Salafi schools may find less ground in the Hanafite way of thinking.

2. Abu Hanifah's links with the Shi'ite school of theology and law, currently predominant in Iran, are exceedingly significant in understanding the extent and depth of the interaction between his school and Shi'ism. Shi'ites take it for granted that Abu Hanifah was a disciple of their doctrinal guru Ja'far-al-Sadiq and believe that Abu Hanifah's methods and approaches to jurisprudence were deeply affected by their leader. However the reputation of Abu Hanifah in the Islamic world as the founder of the largest school of law has overwhelmingly exceeded that of Jafar-al-Sadiq. One must bear in mind that there are details from known Shi'ite sources which verify the learning relationship of Abu Hanifah with al-Sadiq and as a result the idea of a general connection between the Hanifite and Shi'ite schools is heightened.

3. Being a Persian is a distinct feature of Abu Hanifah's character. He is the son of a nation that is currently neighbouring Afghanistan and whose language has had a deep impact on the historical and cultural progress of the whole region. This is particularly important with regards to a conceivable mutual relationship of the Taliban with Iran.

Having said that, the Hanafites, in their broad horizons of national and cultural zones, are not representing an intact unity in beliefs and methods of life and understanding. While the Hanafites in the western part of the Islamic world stand for a more traditional glimpse of their Imam's theological legacy, some Hanafites in India, Pakistan and Afghanistan have indicated an inclination towards a more orthodox approach to religious issues close to that of Hanafites who have traditionally espoused Wahhabism with, the clearest example being Saudi Arabia. This has mainly been the result of a series of historical developments that evolved around the interrelation and interaction between various fluxes of Islamic thought in the region. A prominent culmination of this interface has been the establishment of the Deoband School, Arabic Dar-ul-Ulum ("House of Learning"). This has been the leading Muslim theological center (*madrasah*) of India for more than a century. It was founded in 1867 by Muhammad Subbed Essay in the Saharanpur district of Uttar Pradesh. The theological position of Deoband has always been severely influenced by the 18th-century Muslim reformer Shah Wali Allah and the early 19th-century Indian Wahhabism (Wahhabbyah), gave it a very puritanical and orthodox outlook. The program of studies is highly traditional with pressing emphasis on jurisprudence (*fiqh*), Quranic exegesis (*tafsir*), the study of traditions (*Hadith*), scholastic theology (*kalam*), and philosophy (*falsafah*). Modern disciplines, which are not relevant to a proper knowledge of Islam and can lead to sinful innovation (*bidaah*), have always been looked at with cynicism and therefore overlooked. Likewise, attempts made by reformers to revise the School's curriculum have faced uncompromising resistance on the part of conservative veterans. The modern practice of Islam is studied only in order to purify it of unorthodox accretions. Deoband has produced generations of scholars who spread across the world in various scholarly capacities such as preaching, teaching, judgement and leadership of prayers. Some of these graduates founded academic establishments with identical or hugely similar patterns to those of Deoband, particularly in neighbouring Pakistan. The independence of Pakistan, due purely to its Islamic identity and mass immigration of Muslim population, gave rise in quality and quantity to Islamic centers of learning in Pakistan. Naturally, this led the interested in Dar-ul-Ulum who could not afford to join it to find these Pakistan based centers as legitimate replacements. A considerable number of Afghan religious scholars are, as a matter of fact, graduates of these centers in Pakistan. The students are normally and indiscriminately sponsored by the school for as long as their studies last. This has been the cause for financially challenged students to seek fulfilment of their future ambitions. These students are prepared mainly for religious leadership of the Muslim community. Deoband's enrolment of its students is from all parts of the Muslim world. The Madrasah boasts a library of 69,000 printed books and manuscripts in Arabic, Persian, and Urdu. A mosque, lecture halls, and student residences further serve the scholarly community.

Students, Schools, and Curricula

The word 'Taliban' literally mean "students" in Arabic. However, in Persian this plural form of "talib" means "religious student". The word is merely applied to those who seek religious scholarship in traditional circles of learning, namely madrasahs. The students enrolled in theological and Islamic studies in modern universities are not called "talib". Therefore in this study some words on madrasahs are not out of context. This may provide a picture of the place where the mentality of religious students is basically shaped.

The elementary school for Muslim boys and in some cases girls is called the *kattab* (Arabic for "school"). Another term for it is *maktab*. The earliest of these schools used simple Arabic poetry and proverbs as texts for teaching reading. The methods of teaching have been various in *maktabs* depending on historical stages and geographical locations, yet there has always been a strong emphasis on reading and memorising the Quran, as well as traditions transmitted from the Prophet and eminent pioneers of Islam. Schooling in the elementary form might continue up to age 15. Traditional sayings of the Prophet Muhammad and His disciples have always played a crucial part in formulating the educational agenda of these schools. These sayings are usually looked upon as the chief source of interpretation of legislative, ethical, theological and social laws and rules. In many cases where there is a lack of explicit Quranic texts, these sayings bridge the gap. The truth of the matter is that since there is a consensus among all Muslims concerning any single Quranic text, the theological disputes have historically been a product of alternative interpretation, which in turn predominantly results in various methods of approach to these sayings. Therefore every madrasah, depending on its theological affiliation, promotes certain ways of dealing with these sayings. Nonetheless, in schools where advanced studies are not pursued and concentration is mostly on elementary stages these sayings are only used for moral application and proper conduct without going too deeply into considerations pertinent to their authenticity.

In 20th century Islamic states government-supported primary schools for general instruction tended to displace the *kattab*. Advanced schooling included further study of the Quran, the *Hadith*, and Muslim law.

Traditionally, each mosque is also a school. Leaders, or imams, teach the faithful in discussions and through preaching. Some early mosques built large libraries that aided the cause of public education in their neighbourhoods. Formal mosque schools developed around recognised teachers.

The first real institution of higher learning was the Muslim Academy for Higher Education in Baghdad, opened in 1066-67. This and later centers of higher education were designed mainly for the teaching of orthodox doctrines. Today there are a number of leading Muslim institutions of higher education that stand out. One of them, and perhaps the most famous in the Sunnite world, is Al Azhar University in Cairo, Egypt. Built as a mosque and college by members of the Shi'ite branch of Islam in 970, it became a full university during the 13th century. The university was modernised and expanded in 1961 and attracts students throughout the Islamic world. The Shi'ite counterpart of Al-Azhar is the Najaf institution in Iraq which has lost some significance in the last twenty years due to political circumstances in Iraq and also increasing growth of its Iranian rival Qum. This institution cannot be described as a university in real terms. It comprises a number of schools that more or less pursue the same curricula.

Madrasah is normally a more specialised *maktab* and has long functioned as a seminary for the study of theology and law. Some of these schools also teach grammar, literature, philosophy, mathematics, and natural sciences. It was the great achievement of the madrasah to collect and translate the culture of ancient Greece and later to transmit it to Europe during the late Middle Ages. By introduction of modern and somewhat secular concepts such as new systems of education, which at times included even theology in state organised and maintained institutions, the Muslim traditionalists felt challenged. The reaction was to keep the old styles of learning and to respond through political pressures on their governments. They believed the newly introduced systems were wrong in all dimensions including academic material, teaching styles and most importantly the way by which the teachers would be selected. They proclaimed their belief that a teacher must be selected not merely on the basis of his teaching qualifications but also through his commitment to religious values. They stated that the sprit of Islam must prevail in the whole process of teaching regardless of the subject. However, the *ulema's* attempt to restore the glories of madrasahs were futile due largely to their failure to furnish an adequate replacement to advanced patterns of natural and technological studies introduced by modern systems. Consequently the educational activities of madrasahs became contracted to studies of a purely religious nature. Notwithstanding, the *ulema* were not prepared at all to admit defeat and promulgated that 'the knowledge divined from revelation (meaning scholastic study of religion) is superior to that of experimental acquisition (meaning the natural sciences).' According to their teachings, The Quran and Holy Sayings contain the solutions to political, economic and social dilemmas, and statesmen are required to seek the advice of the *ulemas* and their approval in order to render their administration legitimate in the religious sense. Despite this, with the progress of technology, schools are attempting to become equipped with facilities such as computers, modern library systems and at times foreign language programs. In Iran, with the flow of wealth and serious challenges faced by the theocratic government, the theological seminaries in Qum embarked on programs aimed at the incorporation of computer technology as well as disciplines like modern sociology and comparative religion in their curricula. Traditional sources of Shi'ite knowledge are now available on compact discs and found on the Web. This is expected to lead to shorter periods of graduation on various levels. Having said that, the study of new academic disciplines is restricted to areas of benefit to Islam. These disciplines must be "adequately" used and the orthodox attitudes must be able to be upheld by them. However, in rural areas and regions where the arrival of modern technology is either expensive or not welcome the old landmarks of the fully-fledged traditional schools are still observable. The main financial resource upon which these schools are traditionally based is voluntary donations of the local population as well as portions of levies collected by higher religious authorities. The power to finance the schools brings a massive influence of those under whose sponsorship the schools function. In poverty stricken areas of the Islamic world, aid from wealthy sponsors such as the Saudis has played a decisive role in the maintenance and survival of the schools.

Although the Islamic religious schools are not bound to follow a fixed set of texts and courses of study, the main items invariably remain the same in all of them. All religious students are expected without exception to learn Arabic. They do so from the earliest stage and continue taking more advanced levels as their general studies progress. It is universally agreed that Arabic is the key to other courses of Islamic learning. Almost all texts of scholarly value are in Arabic. It has also been a tradition for non-Arab scholars to author their works in Arabic in order to bestow upon them an impression of profundity and high scholarship. It is not enough to know how to speak; rather one has to learn how to perfectly comprehend the classical language of the Holy Quran and its sacred sayings. In this context the Arabic grammar is of utmost significance. This grammar has been a subject of deep deliberation and meticulous compilation throughout centuries of Islamic learning. An enormous number of books dealing with universal rules and regulations as well as exceptions extracted from texts belonging to eras close to the Prophet's times bear witness to the fact that Arabic is one of the best deliberated grammars. Al-Suyuti is a well-known title in grammatical studies of the Arabic language and has been for centuries a main text in the traditional seminaries. However, there are other texts of importance such as *Al-Kafiyya* as well as *Sharhi-Jami*, which are still being taught in Pakistan and Afghanistan madrasahs.

Logic is also contained in the academic agenda, but its position is greatly affected by the theological manner and insight of the school on reason and its role in understanding Islam. In Shi'ite schools, where the use of human reason is promoted, logic is a fixed item. In schools where Taliban leaders are assumed to have studied books such as "Logic of Taftazani" and "Sullam al-Ulum" are in use.

More controversial is the study of philosophy. Due to the belief that there is no such thing as Islamic philosophy and that religiously unbinding approaches to philosophical issues pose danger to the innocent minds of students, the eminent *ulema* have banned the teaching and study of philosophy in a considerable number of seminaries across the Islamic world. Nevertheless, in areas where a more relaxed form of Islam is in operation the study of philosophy as a culmination of Islamic thinking which could be used as an auxiliary course is welcome. Philosophy in a restricted form is studied in some madrasahs in Pakistan and Afghanistan. In Sunnite schools, the sayings of the Prophet Mohammad are the centre of attention and students are obliged to memorise them as much as their academic level requires. *Fiqh*, or the laws of the Hanafite School, is the ultimate purpose to which a student has to aspire. These laws are themselves cultivated from historical reflections on the Quranic text and the prophetic sayings by many individuals of excellent knowledge pioneered by Imam Abu Hanifah. All the renowned books dealing with Hanifite laws are looked at with reverence and studied carefully by students at various levels of study.

These schools are said to have been the locations where leading figures of the Taliban movement received their education. It is reported that the Taliban's envoy to the UN, Mr Abdul Hakim is a graduate of Binnori school in Karachi, the movement's representative in Islamabad is also a graduate of Darul 'Ulum of Karachi.

Sources of Influence on the Taliban's Islam

It is a fact that Mohammad's prophetic mission was associated with the establishment of a political government that united the Arabic peninsula. Thus the dispute over the ideal government in Islam is as old as Islam itself. Immediately after the death of the Prophet the eminent Muslims indicated a tremendous confusion concerning the selection of their new leader. Although on the Sunni side of Islam a type of universal agreement was later formed about the way in which the first caliph was selected, this selection was accompanied by a number of serious disputes ever since the Muslims lost their prophet and their first political leader. The second largest Islamic denomination, namely Shi'ism, broke away from the rest of the Islamic community simply because it was not prepared to approve the method by which the selection of the first caliph was conducted. Consequently, there is a deep controversy concerning issues such as selection or election of the leader, the nature of his administration, and the policies which that administration is obliged to pursue.

With the accelerating rate of tension between Iran and the Taliban in late 1998, Mulla Mohammad Umar invited a number of *ulema* of various provinces to convene at a meeting in Kabul to find a solution to the internal and external problems being faced by Afghanistan in the light of the Holy Quran and *Hadith*. Umar proclaimed that "the Ulema-e-Kiraam (the respected scholars of Islam) have always truly guided the Muslims. During the Russian invasion they issued a joint *'fatwa'* against the Russians. Now the need of the time is that, repeating their history, they should provide true guidance to the Islamic government and the Afghan public." Three thousand scholars were reported to have gathered in the capital to deliberate upon a 6 point *'istifta'* (religious inquiry) made by Umar. He asked the *Ulema*: (1) In case of an attack by Iran or any other country, will the ensuing war be called *'jihad-fi-sabilillah'* (a holy war) or not? (2) Will the defence of the country be a *'fardh'* (compulsion) upon

the Taliban only or upon each and every citizen? (3) In case of an
attack upon Afghanistan, what will be the duty imposed by Islam
upon the world of Muslims and Muslim governments? (4) Will
defence of the country be enough or will action against the aggressor,
carrying the war to its own territory, be necessary? (5) He added
that the Taliban–implemented Islamic system is under severe
criticism today requesting the *ulema's* opinion whether the system
implemented by the Taliban, i.e., the rules of '*hudood*' and '*qisaas*'
(the Islamic system of chastisement), the department of '*amr-bil-
m`aroof wa nahi `anil munkar* (ordering the good and forbidding
the evil from Islamic view), and other Islamic laws have been
invented by the Taliban or are they established by the Holy Qur'an
and Sunnah, and furthermore, is it the same system which had been
implemented during the *Khilafat-e-Rashidah* (righteous government
of the Prophets first four successors)? (6) The foreign countries
allege that the people of Afghanistan are not happy with the Taliban
government and that they are ruling the country by force, is that
true?

This kind of relationship between the ruler and the scholars is
certainly not influenced by the Iranian example of the Islamic
government in which the supreme religious leader is in full charge.
The Iranian leader, though selected by a number of *ulema*, does not
need to refer to them in decisions he makes. However, Umar's
relationship with the scholars is not without precedent. This pattern
is clearly visible in the historical relationship between the Saudi
rulers and the Wahhabi *ulema* starting from Ibn Saud, the grand
ancestor of the current House of Saud, until today.

In a visit to Saudi Arabia in the 1980s, I learned that Iranian
commoners trying to kiss the Prophet's tomb were being forbidden
from that by Saudis who spoke Persian fluently. I could not believe
that the Saudi authorities have taken the trouble of investment and
language training purely because they wanted to stop Iranian
pilgrims committing what they considered to be *haram* (forbidden).
To my surprise I discovered a few days later that these Saudis
turned out to be Afghans who were engaged in Saudi universities
concentrating on Islamic studies as students (meaning *de facto*
Taliban). These young men were either immigrants themselves or

sons of immigrants who had fled the civil war in their homeland
and come to attain peace, tranquillity, and, if possible, business in
Saudi Arabia. In a short meeting with one of these students, he said
that they are extremely delighted and lucky to have the chance to
learn about the "True Islam". Although most of the Islamic
denominations believe they are the sole representatives of the "True
Islam", in Saudi Arabia this phrase can only mean "Wahhabism". It
is historically famous of Mohammad ibn Abd al Wahhab and his
disciples that they considered themselves as sole representatives of
the "True Islam" and their *fatwas* excommunicating other Muslims
made it possible for Saudi rulers to invade and conquer lands that
were already being ruled by Muslims. Bearing in mind the Wahhabi
impacts already available in Deobandi schools predominant in the
Pashtun inhabited areas, the striking resemblance between the
formation of the Taliban government and that of Saudi Arabia can
provide the researcher with a useful clue to the theological context
of the Taliban beliefs. Some reflections on a theology which helped
to bring the House of Saud to power and keep them there for decades
can furnish an invaluable recipe for anticipating the political and
theological future of the Taliban.

The political and cultural environment of contemporary Saudi
Arabia has been influenced by Wahhabism as a religious movement
that began in central Arabia in the mid-eighteenth century. This
movement, commonly known as the Wahhabi movement, grew out
of the scholarship and preaching of Mohammad ibn Abd al Wahhab,
a scholar of Islamic jurisprudence who had studied in Iraq and the
Hijaz (the Western part of Arabia) before returning to his native
Najd to preach his message of Islamic reform. Ibn Abd al Wahhab
was expressing concern with the way the people of Najd (the Middle
part of Arabia) engaged in practices he considered polytheistic, such
as praying to saints; making pilgrimages to tombs and special
mosques; venerating trees, caves, and stones; and using votive and
sacrificial offerings. He also expressed concern about what he
viewed as a laxity in adhering to Islamic law and in performing
religious devotions, such as indifference to the plight of widows
and orphans, adultery, lack of attention to obligatory prayers, and
failure to allocate shares of inheritance fairly to women. These are

exactly the same conditions and circumstances which the Taliban claimed to be the cause of their movement.

When Mohammad ibn Abd al Wahhab began to preach against these breaches of Íslamic laws, he characterised customary practices as *jahiliya*, the same term used to describe the ignorance of Arabians before the Prophet and also the very same definition given to the state of Afghan society by the Taliban. Initially, Ibn Abdul Wahhab's preaching encountered opposition, but he eventually came under the protection of a local chieftain named Mohammad ibn Saud with whom he formed an alliance. The endurance of the Wahhabi movement's influence may be attributed to the close association between the founder of the movement and the politically powerful Al Saud in southern Najd. This association between the Al Saud and the Al ash Shaykh, as Mohammad ibn Abd al Wahhab and his descendants came to be known, effectively converted political loyalty into a religious obligation. According to Mohammad ibn Abd al Wahhab's teachings, a Muslim must present a *bayah*, or oath of allegiance, to a Muslim ruler during his lifetime to ensure his redemption after death. The ruler is conversely owed unquestioned allegiance from his people so long as he leads the community according to the laws of God. The whole purpose of the Muslim community is to become the living embodiment of God's laws, and it is the responsibility of the legitimate ruler to ensure that the people know God's laws and live in conformity to them.

Mohammad ibn Saud turned his capital, Ad Diriyah, into a center for the study of religion under the guidance of Mohammad ibn Abd al Wahhab and sent missionaries to teach the reformed religion throughout the peninsula, the gulf, and into Syria and Iraq. Together they began a jihad against what they called the backsliding Muslims of the peninsula. Under the banner of religion, preaching the unity of God and obedience to the just Muslim ruler, the Al Saud by 1803 had expanded their dominion across the peninsula from Mecca to Bahrain, installing teachers, schools, and the apparatus of state power. So successful was the alliance between the Al ash Shaykh and the Al Saud that even after the Ottoman sultan had crushed Wahhabi political authority and had destroyed the Wahhabi capital of Ad Diriyah in 1818, the reformed religion remained firmly planted in the settled districts of southern Najd and Jabal Shammar in the north. It would become the unifying ideology in the peninsula when the Al Saud rose to power again in the next century.

Central to Mohammad ibn Abd al Wahhab's message was the essential oneness of God (*tawhid*). The movement is therefore known by its adherents as *ad dawa lil tawhid* (the call to unity), and those who follow the call are known as *ahl at tawhid* (the people of unity) or *muwahhidun* (unitarians). The word Wahhabi was originally used derogatorily by opponents, but has today become commonplace and is even used by some Najdi scholars of the movement.

Mohammad ibn Abd al Wahhab's emphasis on the oneness of God was asserted in contradistinction to *shirk*, or polytheism, defined as the act of associating any person or object with powers that should be attributed only to God. He condemned specific acts that he viewed as leading to *shirk*, such as votive offerings, praying at saints' tombs and at graves, and any prayer ritual in which the supplicant appeals to a third party for intercession with God. Particularly objectionable were certain religious festivals, including celebrations of the Prophet's birthday, Shi'ite mourning ceremonies, and Sufi mysticism. Consequently, the Wahhabis forbid grave markers or tombs in burial sites and the building of any shrines that could become a locus of *shirk*. This emphasis on purifying religion was clearly remembered when the Taliban took over areas where similar practices were prevalent. There were and are still fears about the future of the great Shrine in Mazar-e-Sahrif and also unique statues of Buddha in Taliban hands.

The extensive condemnation of *shirk* is seen in the Wahhabi movement's iconoclasm, which persisted into the twentieth century, most notably with the conquest of At Taif in the Hijaz. A century earlier, in 1802, Wahhabi fighters raided and damaged one of the most sacred Shi'ite shrines, the tomb of Hussain, the son of Imam Ali and grandson of the Prophet, at Karbala in Iraq. In 1804 the Wahhabis destroyed tombs in the cemetery of the holy men in Medina, which was a locus for votive offerings and prayers to the saints. Similar to Hanafites who follow Abu Hanifah, Wahhabis follow the legal school of Ahmad ibn Hanbal and Wahhabi *ulema* accept the authority only of the Quran and Sunna. The Wahhabi *ulema* reject reinterpretation of the Quran and Sunna in regard to issues clearly settled by the early jurists. By rejecting the validity of reinterpretation, Wahhabi doctrine is at odds with the Muslim reformation movement of the late nineteenth and twentieth centuries. This movement seeks to reinterpret parts of the Quran and Sunna to conform with standards set by the West, most notably standards relating to gender relations, family law, and participatory democracy. However, ample scope for reinterpretation remains for Wahhabi jurists in areas not decided by the early jurists. King Fahd ibn Abd al Aziz Al Saud has repeatedly called for scholars to engage in *ijtihad* (use of rational reasoning) to deal with new situations confronting the modernizing kingdom. This is a clear example of the interaction between the Imam, who is the chief executive leader of the *Umma* and *ulema*. Imams (pious political leaders in the Saudi context) confront issues of a complex nature which have to be fully explained to the *ulema* and they have to help the imam by offering an appropriate response.

The Wahhabi movement in Najd was unique in two respects: firstly, the *ulema* of Najd interpreted the Quran and Sunna very literally and often with a view toward reinforcing parochial Najdi practices; secondly, the political and religious leadership exercised its collective political will to enforce conformity in behavior Mohammad ibn Abd al Wahhab asserted that there were three objectives for Islamic government and society. These objectives have been reaffirmed over the succeeding two centuries in missionary literature, sermons, *fatwa* rulings, and in Wahhabi explications of religious doctrine. According to Mohammad ibn Abd al Wahhab the objectives were "to believe in Allah, enjoin good behaviour, and forbid wrongdoing."

Under Al Saud rule, especially during the Wahhabi revival in the 1920s, governments have shown their capacity and readiness to enforce compliance with Islamic laws and interpretations of Islamic values on themselves and others. The literal interpretations of what constitutes right behaviour according to the Quran and *Hadith* have given the Wahhabis the sobriquet of "Muslim Calvinists." To the Wahhabis, for example, performance of prayer that is punctual, ritually correct, and communally performed not only is urged but publicly required of men. Consumption of wine is forbidden to the believer because wine is literally forbidden in the Quran. Under the Wahhabis, however, the ban extended to all intoxicating drinks and other stimulants, including tobacco. Modest dress is prescribed for both men and women in accordance with the Quran, but the Wahhabis specify the type of clothing that should be worn, especially by women, and forbid the wearing of silk and gold, although the latter ban has been enforced only sporadically. Music and dancing have also been forbidden by the Wahhabis at times, as have loud laughter and demonstrative weeping, particularly at funerals. The Wahhabi emphasis on conformity makes external appearance and behaviour a visible expression of inward faith. Therefore, whether one conforms in dress, in prayer, or in a host of other activities becomes a public statement of whether one is a true Muslim. Because adherence to the true faith is demonstrable in tangible ways, the Muslim community can visibly judge the quality of a person's faith by observing that person's actions. In this sense, public opinion becomes a regulator of individual behaviour. Therefore, within the Wahhabi community, which is striving to be the collective embodiment of God's laws, it is the responsibility of each Muslim to look after the behaviour of his neighbour and to admonish him if he goes astray.

To ensure that the community of the faithful will "enjoin what is right and forbid what is wrong," morals enforcers known as *mutawwiin* (literally, "those who volunteer or obey") have been integral to the Wahhabi movement since its inception. *Mutawwiin* have served as missionaries, as enforcers of public morals, and as "public ministers of the religion" who preach in the Friday mosque. Pursuing their duties in Jeddah in 1806, the *mutawwiin* were observed to be "constables for the punctuality of prayers...with an enormous staff in their hand, (who) were ordered to shout, to scold and to drag people by the shoulders to force them to take part in public prayers five times a day." In addition to enforcing male attendance at public prayer, the *mutawwiin* have also been responsible for supervising the closing of shops at prayer time, for looking out for breaches of public morality such as playing music, smoking, drinking alcohol, having hair that is too long (men) or uncovered (women), and dressing immodestly. *Mutawwiin* correspond to the Taliban Department of "enjoin what is right and forbid what is wrong" with identical functions.

4

Political Infrastructure of the Taliban Rule

Allah's Governments

Hizb-al-Lah is no longer an unfamiliar word to the international community. It literally means "the party of Allah". Although this word gained its popularity through Ayatollah Khomeini's frequent use, it was first used by the Quran itself. Therefore, one is entitled to say that Allah Himself laid the foundations of this party. This party is claimed in the Quran to be "the final triumph" and that its members will achieve final prosperity. To revivalist Muslims, the only legitimate claimants of power are members of this party and subsequently the only person for leading the community is the chairman of this party who represents Allah and as a result would be the best qualified person to execute Allah's will in this material world. That is exactly the reason why pioneering Muslims used the words "caliph" and "caliphate".

The politico-religious state comprising the Muslim community and the lands and peoples under its dominion in the centuries following the death (AD 632) of the Prophet Muhammad, ruled by a Caliph (Arabic khalifah, "successor") who held temporal and sometimes a degree of spiritual authority, grew rapidly during the first two centuries to include most of Southwest Asia, North Africa, and Spain. Dynastic struggles later brought about its decline, and it ceased to exist with the Mongol destruction of Baghdad in 1258. The urgent need for a successor to Muhammad as political leader of the Muslim community was met by a group of Muslim elders in Mecca who designated Abu Bakr, the Prophet's father-in-law, as caliph. Several precedents were set in the selection of Abu Bakr, including that of choosing as caliph a member of the Quraysh tribe. The first four caliphs—Abu Bakr, Umar, Uthman, and Ali— whose reigns constituted what later generations of Muslims would often remember as a golden age of pure Islam, largely established the administrative and judicial organization of the Muslim community and forwarded the policy begun by Mohammad of expanding the Islamic religion into new territories. During the 630s, Syria, Jordan, Palestine, and Iraq were conquered; Egypt was taken from Byzantine control in 645; and frequent raids were launched into North Africa, Armenia, and Persia. The assassination of Uthman and the short caliphate of Ali that followed sparked the first sectarian split in the Muslim community. By 661 Ali's rival Mu'awiyah I, a fellow member of Uthman's Umayyad clan, had wrestled away the caliphate and his rule established the Umayyad caliphate that lasted until 750. Despite the largely successful reign of Mu'awiyah, tribal and sectarian disputes erupted after his death. There were three caliphs between 680 and 685, and only after nearly 20 years of military campaigning did the next one, Abd al-Malik, succeed in re-establishing the authority of the Umayyad capital of Damascus. Abd al-Malik is also remembered for building the Dome of the Rock in Jerusalem. Under his son Al-Walid (705–715), Muslim forces took permanent possession of North Africa, converted the native Berbers to Islam, and overran most of the Iberian Peninsula as the kingdom there collapsed. Progress was also made in the East with settlements in the Indus Valley. Umayyad power had never been firmly seated, however, and the caliphate disintegrated rapidly after the long reign of Hisham (724–743). A serious rebellion broke out against the Umayyads in 747, and in 750 the last Umayyad caliph, Marwan II, was defeated in battle by the followers of the Abbasid family. The Abbasids, descendants of an uncle of Mohammad, owed the success of their revolt in large part to their appeal to various pietistic, extremist, or merely disgruntled groups and in particular to the aid of the Shi'ah, a major dissident party that held that the Caliphate belonged by right to the descendants of Ali. That the Abbasids disappointed the expectations of the Shi'ah by taking the Caliphate for themselves left the Shi'ah to evolve into a sect, permanently hostile to the orthodox Sunni majority, that would periodically threaten the established government by revolt. The first Abbasid caliph, As-Saffah (749-754), ordered the elimination of the entire Umayyad clan. The only Umayyad of note who escaped was Abd ar-Rahman, who made his way to Spain and established an Umayyad dynasty that lasted until 1031. The period of 786–861, and especially the caliphates of Harun (786–809) and Al-Ma'mun (813–833), is counted as the height of Abbasid rule. The eastward orientation of the dynasty was demonstrated by Al-Mansur's removal of the capital to Baghdad in 763 and by the later caliph's policy of marrying non-Arabs and recruiting Turks, Slavs, and other non-Arabs as palace guards. Under Al-Ma'mun, the intellectual and artistic heritage of Persia was cultivated and Persian administrators assumed important posts. After 861, anarchy and rebellion shook the empire. Tunisia and eastern Persia came under the control of hereditary governors who made token acknowledgment of Baghdad's sovereignty. Other provinces became less reliable sources of revenue. The Shi'ah and similar groups, including the Fatimids in North Africa, challenged Abbasid rule on religious as well as political grounds. Abbasid power ended in 945, when the Buyids, a family of rough tribesmen from northwestern Persia, took Baghdad under their rule, but retained the Abbasid caliphs as figureheads. The Samanid dynasty that arose in Khorasan and Transoxiana, as well as the Ghaznavids in Central Asia and the Ganges Basin similarly acknowledged the Abbasid caliphs as spiritual leaders of Sunni Islam. On the other hand, the Fatimids proclaimed a new caliphate in 920 in their capital of Al-Mahdiyah in Tunisia and castigated the Abbasids as usurpers. The Umayyad ruler in Spain, Abd ar-Rahman III, adopted the title of caliph in 928 in opposition to both the Abbasids and the Fatimids. Nominal Abbasid authority was restored to Egypt by Saladin in 1171. By that time, the Abbasids had begun to regain some semblance of their former power as the Seljuq dynasty of sultans in Baghdad, which had replaced the Buyids in 1055, itself began to decay. The caliph An-Nasir (1180-1225) achieved a certain amount of success in dealing diplomatically with various threats from the East, but Al-Mustasiim (1242–58) had no such success and was murdered in the Mongol sack of Baghdad that ended the Abbasid line in that city. A section of the family was invited a few years later to establish a puppet caliphate in Cairo that lasted until 1517, but it exercised no power whatsoever.

Of the caliphates, perhaps the best known to contemporary memory is what is called in the West the Ottoman Empire. The Ottoman Empire, an empire created by Turkish tribes in Anatolia, lasted from the decline of the Byzantine Empire in the 14th century until the establishment of Turkey as a republic in 1922. The current conflict between various factions in today's Balkans dates back to an era where the Ottomans were sovereigns of this area.

The empire was named after Uthman, an amir (prince) in Bithynia who began the conquest of neighboring regions and who founded the empire's dynasty around 1300. The first period of Ottoman history, from 1300 to 1481, was one of almost continuous expansion through war, alliance, and outright purchase of territory. Under Uthman and his successors Orhan (ruled 1324–60), Murad I (1360–89), and Bayezid I (1389-1402), nearly all of Anatolia was conquered. Alliances with various factions within the Byzantine Empire won the Ottomans a foothold in Europe in about 1346, and from Gallipoli they moved into Thrace, Macedonia, Bulgaria, and Serbia. At Kosovo in 1389, Murad defeated the Balkan allies to complete Ottoman domination of that territory. Bayezid further strengthened Ottoman rule and was awarded the title of sultan by the Caliph of Cairo. The rapid advance of Ottoman power attracted the notice of the Tatar leader Timur, however, who turned from his conquest of India to protect his western flank. He defeated an Ottoman army at Ankara in 1402. Timur left as quickly as he had come, but years passed before the Ottomans could resume their conquests. Of Bayezid's four sons, Mohammad I (Mehmed as Turks pronounce it) emerged as sultan in 1413; under him and his successors Murad II (1421–51) and Mehmed II (1451–81), the empire reasserted domination over Europe south of the Danube, vanquishing an army of the Crusades at Varna in 1444. In 1453 Constantinople was taken, and in succeeding years Morea, Trebizond, Bosnia, Albania, the Crimea, and other areas were conquered or annexed. Of the many unique military and administrative forms evolved by the Ottomans, the most notable included the *devsirme* system, whereby Christian youths from the Balkans were drafted and converted to Islam for a lifetime of service. The military arm supplied by the *devsirme* system was the Janissary corps, an infantry group attached to the person of the sultan. Mehmed II developed the practice of requiring all members of the government and army, Turkish or Balkan, Muslim or non-Muslim, to accept the status of personal slave of the sultan. By that means he hoped to ensure the indivisibility of his power, with the entire ruling class sworn to absolute obedience. Under Selim I (1512–20) Ottoman expansion resumed. His defeat of the Mamluks in 1516–17 doubled the size of the empire at a stroke by adding to it Syria, Palestine, Egypt, and Algeria. The reign of his son Suleyman I (1520–66), known in Europe as "the Magnificent," was a golden age of Ottoman power and grandeur. He conquered Hungary from the Habsburgs, annexed Tripoli, extended the empire southeastward through Mesopotamia to the Persian Gulf, and made the Ottoman navy dominant in the eastern Mediterranean. After Suleyman's reign, decline set in. Even though territorial expansion continued yet a while, Murad III (1574–95) conquered the Caucasus and seized Azerbaijan from Iran. Administrative and social weaknesses became insidious. The decline of the empire after Suleyman is attributed to the increasing lack of ability in the sultans who followed him, the ever-increasing power of the *devsirme* class and the tensions it created within the ruling class, the erosion of Ottoman industry, the decline of Ottoman-controlled trade routes with the development of better navigation, and sudden leaps in population and the subsequent decline of urban centers. Reforms instituted in the 17th century were too weak and narrow to arrest the decline. Meanwhile, the powerful nation-states arising in Europe during this period formed alliances to drive the Ottomans off the continent. Decline accelerated in the 18th century, which saw the decay of rural administration into small, feudal-like states and increased unrest in the cities, disrupting food supplies and leading to widespread famine. Few of the innovations in technology that underlaid Europe's prosperity made their way into the empire. Early in the 18th century some aristocrats did adopt Western styles (the Tulip Period), and later in the century Selim II tried to modernize the government. However, in a reactionary revolt led by Mustafa IV in 1807, the empire returned to traditional ways. By the accession of Mahmud II in 1808, the Ottoman situation appeared desperate. Local authorities openly opposed the central government, while the empire was at war with both England and Russia. In the next few decades Mahmud II re-established some order with military modernization and governmental reorganization, but the boundaries of the empire continued to shrink. Mahmud's sons, Abdulmecid I and Abdülaziz, enacted a series of liberal and modernizing reforms called the Tanzimat, which were widely viewed in the West as an effort to encourage friendly relations with European powers. Among the reforms were the first comprehensive education system and the westernisation of commercial, maritime, and penal codes. The centralization of power removed all checks on the power of the emperor, but in 1876 Abdulhamid II agreed to the first constitution in any Islamic country. Two years later, by the Treaty of San Stefano and negotiations at the Congress of Berlin, the empire was forced to give up Romania, Serbia, Montenegro, Bulgaria, Cyprus, and other territories. Abdulhamid was able to hold the empire together for the rest of the century by reminding Europeans that the Turks within their own borders were kept peaceful by its preservation, but the final years of his reign were marked by revolts, notably that of the Young Turks in 1908. The Balkan wars of 1912–13 all but completed the empire's expulsion from Europe. After a disastrous defeat in World War I and a revolution immediately after, the 36th and final Ottoman emperor, Mehmed VI Vahideddin, was overthrown in 1922 and modern Turkey was formed.

With this history of major caliphates in mind, one is entitled to wonder which kind of emirate and caliphate the Taliban plan to enforce. On the one hand they call their domain an emirate, which is apparently at odds with a caliphate in terms of their administrative implications. Historically, 'caliph' was a title granted to those who were assumed to be mainly spiritual successors of the Prophet. That is exactly the reason why the Abbasids, though incapable of maintaining their political powers, were left to keep their caliphate thrones by powerful local rulers who at times expanded their administrative territories even to Baghdad. The caliph could represent Islamic integrity both spiritually and politically. With the emergence of powerful local rulers, the caliph's jurisdiction was restricted to that of spiritual representation. The local rulers were called emirs and at times, depending on their position with caliphs, they would be granted titles such as sultan. Emirs usually sought their religious legitimacy through the approval of the caliphs. Strangely enough the Shi'ite emirs from the Buyid tribe who consolidated their rule over Baghdad did not make arrangements to remove the Sunni caliph who was not seen by them to represent any sort of legitimacy. The collapse of the Abbasid caliphate coincided with the advent of independent emirates that ruled independently from the central spiritual and political power of the caliphs. As a result there emerged various approaches to political power less affected by Islam but mostly shaped by absolutist ambitions and the wisdom of individual rulers.

Contemporary Political Administrations of Allah

With the victory of the Islamic revolution in Iran it was claimed that the first Islamic government after the Ottoman caliphate had come into existence. However, from a Shi'ite point of view inside Iran, based on the illegitimacy of all caliphates after the Prophetic era except for that of Ali, it was the first genuine government of Islam to hold the political administration in 1400 years. Nevertheless, neither the first opinion nor the second appeared to be verifiable by a large number of Muslims who firmly believed that there existed a real Islamic state long before the Islamic Republic of Iran, namely in Saudi Arabia.

With an eye to the fact that the Taliban, by both their kind of Hanifite beliefs and years of association with the Saudi way of life, either in Pakistan or in Saudi Arabia itself, have developed a transparent view of the Saudi political system, and with attention to the predominance of Iranian experience which has inspired the politics of Islam for the last twenty years, one might rightly conclude that the structure of the Taliban's political thought must contain strong impacts from both aforesaid systems.

Iranian Example

The pivotal mechanism to the whole political structure of the Islamic government in Iran is *valy-e faqih*. The preamble to the Constitution vests supreme authority in the *valy-e faqih* (The *faqih* in charge; *faqih*, Shi'ite religious professor). According to the constitution, the *valy-e faqih* is the just and pious jurist who is recognized by the majority of the people at any period as best qualified to lead the nation. In both the preamble and main text of the constitution, Ayatollah Khomeini is recognized as the first *valy-e faqih*. Certain articles specify the qualifications and duties of the *valy-e faqih*. The duties include appointing the jurists to the Council of Guardians; the chief judges of the judicial branch; the chief of staff of the armed forces; the commander of the Pasdaran (*Pasdaran-e Enqelab-e-Islami*, or Islamic Revolutionary Guards Corps, or Revolutionary Guards); the personal representatives of the *valy-e faqih* to the Supreme Defense Council; and the commanders of the army, air force, and navy, following their nomination by the Supreme Defense Council. The *valy-e faqih* is also authorized to approve candidates for presidential elections. In addition, he is empowered to dismiss a president who has been impeached by the Majlis or found by the Supreme Court to be negligent in his duties.

The Constitution also provides procedures for succession to the position of *valy-e faqih*. After Ayatollah Khomeini, the office of *valy-e faqih* was to pass to an equally qualified jurist. If a single religious leader with appropriate qualifications cannot be recognized consensually, religious experts elected by the people are to choose from among themselves three to five equally distinguished jurists who will then constitute an assembly of *valyat-e faqih,* or Leadership Council.

In accordance with the constitution, an eighty-three-member Assembly of Experts was elected in December 1982 to choose a successor to Khomeini. Even before the first meeting of the Assembly of Experts in the spring of 1983, some influential members of the clergy had been trying to promote Ayatollah Hosain Ali Montazeri (born 1923), a former student of Ayatollah Khomeini, as successor to the office of *valy-e faqih*. As early as the fall of

1981, Ayatollah Khomeini himself had indicated in a speech that he considered Montazeri to be the best qualified for the position of *valy-e faqih*. At the third meeting, Montazeri was designated "successor," to Ayatollah Khomeini. However, following dramatic political developments Ayatollah Montazari resigned his post and Ayatollah Ali Khameneii was declared the leader of the Islamic revolution immediately after death of Ayatollah Khomeini.

The Taliban experience in power is to some extent immature in comparison to the twenty year old Iranian government. However, lines of resemblance and discrepancy are already observable.

The similarities could be identified in some main areas:

1. The Taliban Government is not headed by a president or a democratically elected figure in the modern sense.

2. Representing the last Shi'ite Imam (now in occultation), the Iranian leader considers himself to be the deputy of that Imam who in turn is the sole representative of God. The selection of a leader by the elected clergy is not public approval but it is public recognition of the Leader's qualification for succession.

3. The Taliban selection of a leader is basically a responsibility of the *ulema* association.

4. The head of state in a Taliban government enjoys extensive authority and executive powers.

Hypothetically, the discrepancies are considerable. However, one can ignore some of them under practical conditions.

1. Considering the crucial and continuous role of the *ulema* in identifying the ruler and drawing up internal and international policies, it would be technically incorrect to describe the emir or *Amir al-Mu'minin* (the commander of the faithful) as the pivotal structure for the Taliban political system.

2. Receiving his legitimacy from the *ulema*, the Taliban leader must recognize that he is representing the Prophet, whose blessings and approval ought to be sought through the *ulema*. Therefore, he needs to consult them on a regular basis in order to keep religiously justifying the foundation of his decisions.

3. The Taliban have frequently made clear their stand against democracy in its contemporary sense. Ironically enough, in the Iranian example in which the leader is claimed to be representing

the occulted Shi'ite Imam and as a result Allah Himself, and that there is no selection but recognition of the leader, there has been a constant claim on the democratic nature of government.

However, in practical terms, even in the Taliban experience, the role of *ulema* can be restricted to that of providing religious legitimacy with the *Amir al-Muminin* in full charge using his political and financial powers to act freely. A manifestation of this kind of *ulema*-leaders relationship can be found in the Saudi experience which merits consideration in this context.

Saudi Example

Numerous religious inquiries directed to *ulema* concerning various issues, including the legality of killings conducted by the Taliban of their Muslim opponents, remind of an alliance formed between Mohammad ibn Abd al Wahhab and Mohammad ibn Saud, the grand ancestor of the House of Saud. The similar backgrounds and the intellectual and educational links of the Taliban with Saudi Arabia make the study of developments of the aforesaid alliance invaluable. This study facilitates the procedure of examining the Taliban religio-political doctrine. Similar to Afghanistan, the political and cultural environment of contemporary Saudi Arabia itself was tremendously influenced by a religious movement that began in central Arabia in the mid-eighteenth century. This movement, commonly known as the Wahhabi movement, grew out of the scholarship and preaching of Mohammad ibn Abd al Wahhab.

Mohammad ibn Abd al Wahhab was concerned with the way the people of Najd engaged in practices he viewed as polytheistic, such as praying to allegedly sacred people; making pilgrimages to tombs and special temples; revering trees, caves, and stones; and using votive and sacrificial offerings. He was also concerned by what he viewed as a slackness in conforming to Islamic law and in performing religious devotions, such as unresponsiveness to the predicament of vulnerable members of their community, adultery, lack of attention to obligatory prayers, and failure to allocate shares of inheritance fairly.

When Mohammad ibn Abd al Wahhab commenced preaching his message and speaking against these violations of Islamic laws, he characterized customary practices as *jahiliya*. Initially, Abd al Wahhab's preaching encountered opposition, but he eventually came under the protection of Muhammad ibn Saud, with whom he formed an alliance. The endurance of the Wahhabi movement's influence may be attributed to the close association between the founder of the movement and the politically powerful Al Saud in southern Najd.

This alliance between the Al Saud and the Al ash Shaykh, as Muhammad ibn Abd al Wahhab and his descendants came to be known, effectively converted political loyalty into a religious obligation. According to Mohammad ibn Abd al Wahhab's teachings, a Muslim must present a *bayah*, or oath of allegiance, to his contemporary Muslim rulers during his lifetime to ensure his redemption after death. The ruler, conversely, is owed unquestioned loyalty from his people so long as he leads the community according to the laws of God. The whole purpose of the Muslim community is to become the living embodiment of God's laws, and it is the responsibility of the legitimate ruler to ensure that people know God's laws and live in conformity to them.

Mohammad ibn Saud turned his capital, Ad Diriyah, into a center for the study of religion under the guidance of Muhammad ibn Abd al Wahhab and sent missionaries to teach the reformed religion throughout the peninsula, the Gulf, and into Syria and Mesopotamia. Together they began a jihad against the backsliding Muslims of the peninsula. Under the banner of religion, and preaching the unity of God and obedience to the just Muslim ruler, the Al Saud by 1803 had expanded their dominion across the peninsula from Mecca to Bahrain installing teachers, schools, and the apparatus of state power. So successful was the alliance between the Al ash Shaykh and the Al Saud that even after the Ottoman sultan had crushed Wahhabi political authority and had destroyed the Wahhabi capital of Ad Diriyah in 1818, the reformed religion remained firmly planted in the settled districts of southern Najd and of Jabal Shammar in the north. It would become the unifying ideology in the peninsula when the Al Saud rose to power again in the next century.

Under Al Saud rule, governments, especially during the Wahhabi revival in the 1920s, have shown their capacity and readiness to enforce compliance with Islamic laws and interpretations of Islamic values on themselves and others.

As such, this alliance, if appropriately organized and utilized, could gain the Taliban the highest of their political ambitions in an area populated by a Sunni *ulema*-abiding population. The example of a Hanifite puritan government could and has raised hopes even among Pakistanis who wish to see this force come up against their regional contenders.

The Taliban Socio-Political Doctrine

The Taliban have often repeated their concern with social stability as an effective solution to other problems. They have also made it clear that they are determined to achieve law and order in society through Islamic ways. It has now transpired that they are not sympathetic with newly established psychological solutions which encourage patience and understanding in social dilemmas. Instead, they have laid the foundations of an institution which they believe to have it's roots in the Holy Quran. The following report by *Dharb-i-Mu'min* may shed some light on the operational performance of this institution.

Afghanistan's *Amr bil M'aroof* (enjoin the good) department has hanged three people who, in the guise of the Taliban, had committed robberies in Mazar-e-Sharif. The three were hanged to death after the Sharee`at Court had carried out full investigations and found them guilty. The *'Amr bil M'aroof wa nahi anil munkar'* (enjoin the good and forbid the evil) department, soon after its establishment in the recently captured Mazar-e-Sharif, has demonstrated its efficiency in capturing the culprits. After receiving a tip off last week, the workers of the *Amr bil M'aroof* department in a raid arrested three robbers who had disguised themselves as the Taliban. They had entered people's homes on the pretext of a search and robbed them of their valuables. During the investigations the culprits confessed having robbed many people. They admitted having murdered a number of people, as well as holding some to ransom. After

carrying out a thorough investigation into their crimes, the Sharee`at
Court sentenced them to death. The case was then heard in High Court.
Eye-witnesses testified against the three criminals. Their guilt having
been proved by Shara`ee evidence, Mulla Nooruddin Turabi, presiding
over the case passed the verdict of death by hanging. Thus on Monday
the three criminals were hanged to death separately; in Mazar-e-Sharif,
the capital of the Balkh province Shiberghan, the provincial capital of
Jowzjan, and Saripul. The Afghan Chief Justice Mulla Nooruddin
Turabi, Governor of Balkh Mulla `Abdul Mannan Niazi and Interior
Minister Mulla Khairullah Khairkhwa were present at the hangings.
Dharb-i-Mu'min was informed that this was the first time the Taliban
had enforced the rule of *Hadd* in the northern areas. The public hangings
will have far-reaching consequences it is being hoped. The enforcement
of Shara`ee laws will go a long way in establishing peace and security
in the area. In all three cities thousands of people watched the sentence
being carried out. Maulvi `Abdul Rahman, head of the Department of
'*Amr bil M'aroof*' in the northern areas, informed the people that the
three men had been found guilty of such heinous crimes as murders and
kidnappings.

In another story Dharb said:

Governor of Laghman Province Mulla Noorullah Noori, expressing deep
satisfaction on the law and order situation in the province, has said that
it is due to the arrival of the Taliban that the people of the entire area
are leading calm and peaceful daily lives with deep mutual love and
understanding. Providing an insight to our correspondent, the Governor
said that in the last two years only a single person had been sentenced
to death according to the rules of *Qisaas* (certain Islamic code of
punishment). And this *Qisaas* had turned the province, known for its
lawlessness, into a haven of peace and harmony. This was not less than
a miracle, Mulla Noorullah said, for a people deadly enemies of each
other, have forgotten all their differences and enmity and are living
calm and congenial peaceful lives. Mulla Noorullah went on to explain
that all the government departments, those of education, health,
communications, agriculture, reconstruction were fully operational and
functioning satisfactorily. He said that the provincial department of
Amr bil M'aroof wa nahi anil munkar was the most comprehensive
department, controlling the workings of all other departments, and
providing religious guidance to the people. The said department was

actively working for the betterment of the people. The governor added that the people of the province were gladly co-operating with the Taliban administration.

Creation of this department delineates the supremacy of religious affairs over all other facets of civil life. This is a fact indicated by Mulla Noorullah in his above statement. Therefore, a special stance must be recognized for this department and its operational plan in the whole political structure of the Taliban government. However, the nature of the Department's link to the political leadership of the Taliban remains a matter of ambiguity and only the forthcoming developments would help present a more transparent picture of that relationship. The fact that the Department, in conducting its duties, depends fundamentally on *ulema* both in policy and administration. The Department's regulations, though partly known through its conduct, have not been brought to public access in writing. The Taliban policy to monitor and enforce religious regulations by members of the public, including the main gender issues, has raised controversy and resentment in the outside world. However, this system is not unprecedented and as previously indicated there was a pattern to look at and to follow by the Taliban, namely the Saudi experience on the matter. The Taliban's message is similar to that of pioneering Saudis and the Taliban seem to be determined to get that message through. Even the way the Taliban want to convey that message is amazingly analogous, if not identical, with that of the Wahhabis. Like Mohammad ibn Abd al Wahhab, central to the Taliban's message was the essential oneness of God (*tawhid*). Again similar to the Taliban, Mohammad ibn Abd al Wahhab's emphasis on the oneness of God was asserted in contradistinction to *shirk*, or polytheism, defined as the act of associating any person or object with powers that should be attributed only to God. Ibn Abd al Wahhab condemned specific acts that he viewed as leading to *shirk*, such as votive offerings, praying at saints' tombs and at graves, and any prayer ritual in which the suppliant appeals to a third party for intercession with God. Particularly objectionable were certain religious festivals, including celebrations of the Prophet's birthday, Shi'ites mourning ceremonies, and Sufi mysticism. Consequently, the Wahhabi forbid grave markers or tombs in burial sites and the building of any shrines that could become a locus of *shirk*.

The extensive condemnation of *shirk* is seen in the movement's iconoclasm, which persisted into the twentieth century, most notably with the conquest of At Taif in the Hijaz. A century earlier, in 1802, Wahhabi fighters raided and damaged one of the most sacred Shi'ah shrines, the tomb of Husayn, the son of Imam Ali and grandson of the Prophet, at Karbala in Iraq. In 1804 the Wahhabis destroyed tombs in the cemetery of the holy men in Medina, which was a locus for votive offerings and prayers to the saints. Although sympathetic in beliefs with Wahhabis, the Taliban have tried to avoid the consequences of such drastic actions. However, reported massacres of Shi'ites and the demolishing of sacred tombs have pushed forwards concerns regarding the possibility of further engagement of the Taliban in such actions in a more dramatic fashion.

Following the legal school of Ahmad ibn Hanbal, Wahhabi *ulema* accept the authority only of the Quran and Sunna. The Wahhabi ulema reject reinterpretation of the Quran and Sunna in regard to issues clearly settled by the early jurists. By rejecting the validity of reinterpretation, Wahhabi doctrine is at odds with the Muslim reformation movement of the late nineteenth and twentieth centuries which seeks to reinterpret parts of the Quran and Sunna to conform with standards set by the West, most notably standards relating to gender relations, family law, and participatory democracy. So is the Taliban movement within the Hanifite school of law. However, ample scope for reinterpretation remains for Wahhabi jurists in areas not decided by the early jurists.

The Wahhabi movement in Najd was unique in two respects: firstly, the *ulema* of Najd interpreted the Quran and Sunna very literally and often with a view toward reinforcing parochial Najdi practices; secondly, the political and religious leadership exercised its collective political will to enforce conformity in behavior. Mohammad ibn Abd al Wahhab asserted that there were three objectives for Islamic government and society. These objectives have been reaffirmed over the succeeding two centuries in missionary literature, sermons, *fatwa* rulings, and in Wahhabi explications of religious doctrine. According to Mohammad ibn Abd al Wahhab the objectives were "to believe in Allah, enjoin good behavior, and forbid wrongdoing."

Under Al Saud rule, governments, especially during the Wahhabi revival in the 1920s, have shown their capacity and readiness to enforce compliance with Islamic laws and interpretations of Islamic values on themselves and others. The literal interpretations of what constitutes right behavior according to the Quran and *Hadith* have given the Wahhabis the sobriquet of "Muslim Calvinists." To the Wahhabis, for example, performance of prayer that is punctual, ritually correct, and communally performed not only is urged but publicly required of men. Consumption of wine is forbidden to the believer because wine is literally forbidden in the Quran. Under the Wahhabis, however, the ban extended to all intoxicating drinks and other stimulants, including tobacco. Modest dress is prescribed for both men and women in accordance with the Quran, but the Wahhabis specify the type of clothing that should be worn, especially by women, and forbid the wearing of silk and gold, although the latter ban has been enforced only sporadically. Music and dancing have also been forbidden by the Wahhabis at times, as have loud laughter and demonstrative weeping, particularly at funerals.

The Wahhabi emphasis on conformity makes of external appearance and behavior a visible expression of inward faith. Therefore, whether one conforms in dress, in prayer, or in a host of other activities becomes a public statement of whether one is a true Muslim. Because adherence to the true faith is demonstrable in tangible ways, the Muslim community can visibly judge the quality of a person's faith by observing that person's actions. In this sense, public opinion becomes a regulator of individual behavior. Therefore, within the Wahhabi community, which is striving to be the collective embodiment of God's laws, it is the responsibility of each Muslim to look after the behavior of his neighbor and to admonish him if he goes astray.

To ensure that the community of the faithful will "enjoin what is right and forbid what is wrong," morals enforcers have been integral to the Wahhabi movement since its inception. The religious police have served as ministers of religion, as enforcers of public morals, and as "parameters of right and wrong" who preach in the Friday mosque. Pursuing their duties in Jeddah in 1806, these people were described as "constables for the punctuality of prayers"...In a similar way to that of workers of righteousness in the Taliban administration, the Saudi pioneering religious enforcement police, with an enormous staff in their hand, were ordered to shout, to scold and to drag people by the shoulders to force them to take part in public prayers five times a day. In addition to enforcing male attendance at public prayer, these morals promoters were also responsible for supervising the closing of shops at prayer time, for looking out for infringements of public morality such as playing music, smoking, drinking alcohol, having hair that is too long (men) or uncovered (women), and dressing immodestly.

There might be various reasons why the presence of a force specialized in spreading Islamic morality in its above form has not been among the institutional changes introduced to Iran after the Islamic revolution. The fact is that morality enforcement is a task referred to as a compulsory religious duty in the Quran and as a result there existed a good deal of enthusiasm for it in the Iranian Revolution. However, the methods developed and used by Muslim revolutionaries in Iran bear little resemblance to those of Wahhabis in Saudi Arabia.

The Taliban and Democracy

As quoted previously, the *ulema's* role in the structure of power within the Taliban administration is technically superior to that of a leader. The *ulema's* attitudes towards local and international issues are central to governmental approaches to these issues. The general impression of the traditionalist *ulema* who opposed reformist movements was and still is one of suspicion towards political, economic and philosophical notions born and fostered in the West. One of these notions is, no doubt, democracy. Despite a profound disagreement within scholarly circles of Islam, there is a semi-consensus on the illegitimacy of a political administration which does not represent Allah. Even a democratically elected government has to be in one way or another representative of Islamic divine legitimacy. However, for Muslim theologians the enigma is whether or not the ballot boxes could reveal the will of Allah, and if the performance of the elected government is echoing the Perfect Divine Wisdom or the vulnerabilities of the creatures. Practically, there arises another dilemma, that is to say that if the *ulema* accept in principal that Muslim public opinion represented by an elected government is identical with the Divine Will, then what would the role of the *ulema* be in interpretation and reflection of that Will. In a long-standing dispute over Islamic acceptability of democracy and its related issues, it seems that traditionalists emphatically deny Islam's preparedness to acknowledge the right of people to have the final say. As a result the *ulema* do not compromise the Divine Voice of which they are the only lawful speakers. The following statement issued by Mufti Rasheed Ahmad Sahib helps identify the anti-democracy oriented theology of the revivalist Islam in Afghanistan.

Allah Ta'ala cannot be thanked enough for having blessed, after centuries, the oppressed Muslim *Ummah* with a Khilafat-Rashidah (righteous caliphate) form of Government; an Islamic Shara'ee Government and authority.

Today, thanks to Allah Ta'ala, we are very fortunate that under the leadership of the *Ameer-ul-Mu'mineen* the Talaba (students) of religious Madaris (schools) have written down history with their pious blood and exemplary sacrifices, and have thus gladdened our hearts and souls. By practically implementing the laws of Islam, our proud and blessed sons have proved wrong the propaganda of the Christians and Jews that the Quran and *Hadith* system of government has become outdated and thus impossible to be put to practical use. Alas! The weaker Muslims were also coming to believe this ridiculous propaganda, and were thus going astray. The implementation of Islam had become a thing of the past. People calling themselves Muslims, were using Islam for their own personal motives. Islam was being used by them as a form of politics. Even the leaders of the fourteen years of jihad who had in Kabul acquired power, strength and dignity instead of implementing the true Islam began presenting a pseudo-Islam; so much that they started affixing such anti-Islam terms as 'democracy', 'president', 'prime-minister', 'elections', and 'caretaker president' to Islam. They started including in Islam the ways and manners of Europe and America.

The elements of resentment that follow the European and American ways is transparently clear in the above passage. One must take note of the fact that with the consolidation of the Taliban power in Afghanistan, the idea of a total break away from anything Western will definitely be amplified.

The failure of previous Islamic movements that sought to seize political power through the incorporation of so-called modern reforms and the incapability of parties like *Rifah* in Turkey to maintain their stability in power against attacks waged by their secularist rivals provide the Islamic activists with further reason to put faith in the Taliban's uncompromising experience based on the aforesaid traditional point of view.

5

The Taliban and Economy

It would be hard to imagine as to how a country with a poorly administered economy could set an example in political and cultural excellence for the rest of the world. The problem of economic under-achievement in the Islamic world has long provoked heated disputes over causes and reasons. This question is usually treated by Muslim activists as a secondary issue and a side effect of cultural conflict between the West and the Islamic world. The Taliban will be in no position to innovate solutions to Afghanistan's economy except through a careful study of what already exists in terms of Islamic theories, explanations and experimental lessons.

Economic Development and the Islamic World

Believing in the supremacy of Islamic culture, the goal of Muslim countries and Islamic movements throughout the last several decades has been "economic development". The first priority of the governments and parties within the Islamic world, with various approaches, is that they should progress more and more economically, and do so fast so that they stand soonest at par with the developed, well-off and culturally rival nations. Apparently, there seems nothing wrong with such thinking, yet it is a matter of deep contemplation.

There are two questions which are central and require well-studied answers from Muslim Scholars.

1. If the development experience of the Muslim countries in particular and of the Third World countries in general, as it is, over

the last 40 to 50 years has failed to inaugurate a new era of sustained growth and widespread well-being, can there be an alternate road?

2. If Muslim economists believe that capitalist as well as socialist roads have landed mankind into a cul-de-sac, is there a way out?

Muslims claim they have an alternative. Islam is not merely a religion that deals with private relationship between man and God, it provides guidance for the entire gamut of life, including man's economic life and destiny.

The 'deity' that has been light-heartedly adored in the post Second World War era, both in economically rich and politically prosperous countries of the West as well as in the poverty stricken and newly independent countries of the ex-colonial empires in Asia and Africa, has been the 'deity' of development. As the German scholar, Wolfgang Sachs, concisely puts:

"The last 40 years can be called the age of development... Like a towering lighthouse, guiding sailors towards the coast, 'development' stood as the idea that oriented emerging nations in their journey through post-war history. No matter whether democracies or dictatorships, the countries of the South proclaimed development as their primary aspiration, after they had been freed from colonial subordination. Four decades later, governments and citizens alike still have their eyes fixed on this light flashing just as far away as ever: every effort and every sacrifice is justified in reaching the goal, but the light keeps on receding into the dark... Since then the relations between North and South have been cast in this mould: 'development' provided the fundamental frames of reference for that mixture of generosity, bribery and oppression that has characterised the policies towards the South. For almost half a century, good neighbourliness on the planet was conceived in the light of 'development'."

"The scenario is now changing today," adds Wolfgang Sachs, "the lighthouse shows cracks and is starting to crumble. The idea of development stands like a ruin in the intellectual landscape." In fact, "this epoch is coming to an end. The time is ripe to write its obituary." Muslim scholars whose views are vastly reflected in the hearts and minds of the Muslim population have always been cynical and warned against the insufficiency of the so-called economic ideals. To them obituaries have started appearing.

The First Global Revolution, a report by the Council of the Club of Rome, is one recent obituary from an international think-tank. The report of the United Nations Development Programme, Human Development Report 1992 is another obituary, written in a somewhat different vein. The Club of Rome intellectuals start with the lament: "Humankind seems to be gripped by a *fin de siècle* attitude of uncertainty at the threshold of the new century, but the era of a millennium brings still deeper mystique with its sense of widespread change and the uncertainty accompanying it."

The results of developmental efforts, the report regretfully confesses, "have been uneven and often disappointing" and warns "the grave problems of world poverty, aggravated by population growth, could well give rise to great and disruptive disharmony on a wide scale, from which the industrial countries cannot escape the consequences." The report suggests that "it is strongly in the self-interest of the rich countries that a new, powerful and radically different approach be taken to the problems of world development."

The Human Development Report 1992 brings to focus the glaring reality that the rich have grown richer and the poor become poorer at the end of the three decades of the so-called universal developmental effort. In 1960 wealthiest one billion of the world's five billion population were 30 times better off than the poorest one billion. According to the latest estimates, taking into account internal discrepancies within nations, the top one fifth are probably around 150 times better off. *The Guardian* editorially comments that the "developing countries enter the market as unequal partners and leave with unequal shares."

Although the editorial falls short of calling this act of penalisation of the Third World by "international economists and financiers" an attempt "to defraud the developing countries," it does accept that through "what is at best self-deception these actions have the same result." The tragic consequence is that "for a sizeable slice of the world's population, three decades of much-trumpeted development have been three decades of de-development." (April 25, 1992)

The condition within the rich and developed countries is no different. About the US some relevant information released by the Congressional Budget Office shows that the richest one percent of the population got almost 70 percent of the increase in average family income between 1977 and 1989. The situation becomes more startling if the income rise of the richest 20 percent is taken during this period. The richest 20 percent took more than 100 percent of the growth in average income with the result that the bottom 40 percent of the population actually lost ground and transferred part of what they were getting 15 years back to the richest 20 percent. See "To Close the Wealth Gap," *The New York Times* editorial reproduced in *The International Herald Tribune*, April 23, 1992.

This is the global context, in which we are reviewing the development "syndrome". In short, this is reliable evidence used by Muslim reformers and revivalists to verify their claim that the Islamic world has to break away from the fashionable economics of the West.

Man has always been searching for short cuts to realise his ideals. With political freedom, the Third World's self-realisation of its economic and social plight deepened. Its exposure to the West made it even more conscious of its abject poverty and of the widening gap between the rich and the poor. During the era of colonial rule, the Third World heard many success stories of western development. In the post-colonial period it was invited to follow the growth path pursued by the West. Economic development was offered to the people of the Third World as an answer to all their problems.

In the pursuit of development, industrialisation was seen as "the quick way to prosperity" and capital formation was emphasised as the key to industrialisation. Transfer of western technology and foreign aid were seen as sufficient to make up for the two major gaps in savings and balance of payments. Import-substitution and, to a lesser extent, export-promotion strategies were developed to realise the dream. Economic development became the new deity at whose altar everything else was to be sacrificed—values, cultural patterns, social norms, customs, religion, ethics and what not. It was assumed that a rising GNP would usher in a new age of prosperity and affluence. Mankind would enter a new millennium of affluence by following in the footsteps of the developed countries of the West.

These conclusions may rightly be described as rather too simplistic. But Muslims argue that it is equally true that the development strategies based on western models, as they were introduced in the Third World, contained a host of simplifications, carefully wrapped in sophisticated jargon, and not without an element of arrogance about the superiority of the western way of life. The most positive, even enthusiastic, response came from the Third World's western-educated elite, who had been brought up in the cradle of colonialism and had inherited power from the departing masters. This alliance of convenience between the West and the new power-elite of the Third World is now under severe strain because the development strategy that was diligently pursued has failed to produce the required results. In almost every developing country, indigenous forces not so favourably disposed towards the western models are engaged in a search for new paths more in keeping with their own cultural identity. They are challenging the westernising minority almost everywhere.

Even if it is conceded that too many hopes were pinned on the drama of development, the record of the last 30 years is still disappointing. The problems of poverty, underdevelopment and stagnation continue unameliorated. Two centuries after the advent of the industrial revolution and three decades after the inauguration of a grandiose development crusade, it is disturbing to note that a majority of the human race remains poor, suffering from under-nourishment, under-shelter, disease and illiteracy. The World Bank acknowledged with regret that the failure to achieve a minimum level of income above the "poverty line" has kept some 40 percent of the populations of the less developed countries in a condition of "absolute poverty."

Although some "enclaves" of development have emerged as a result of developmental efforts, they have failed to result in any broad-based changes in the society; nor were they able to mobilise all major sectors of society in the cause of development. Over-emphasis on capital has generated distortions in price structure, exchange rates, tax system, wage-scales, forms of technology and so on. Distributional aspects have been largely ignored with the result that economic and social disparities within societies have increased. Employment-generating effects have been far below the required minimum. Even natural population increase and consequent inflow in the labour force could not be absorbed in the economy through new employment opportunities. In spite of import-substitution strategies, dependence on imports continues and, as terms of trade have generally moved against the developing countries, trade and balance-of-payments gaps have increased. International indebtedness has also rocketed while the net flow of real resources from the developed countries to the Third World has not only tapered off, in some cases even a reverse flow has begun. The energy crisis has further aggravated the resource constraints. The overall picture remains bleak.

A word may also be added about the international context in which developmental efforts of the Third World countries have taken place. The relation of dependence that was built into international economic relations during the colonial period continues unabated. The gap between the rich and the poor nations is widening. Prices of internationally traded goods show erratic movements injurious to the interests of the developing countries. Inflation is being aggravated by the monetary and trade policies of the developed countries. Twenty of the 24 developed countries are pursuing protectionist policies *vis-à-vis* imports from the Third World. Consequently Third World countries are caught in severe balance-of-payments problems. International monetary institutions are unable to handle the situation. The UNDP study, Human Development Report 1992, accepts that the structure and working of the World Bank and IMF must undergo fundamental changes if they are to be responsive to the needs of the poorer countries of the world. Crises are being postponed, not controlled. The fate of development in the Third World is very much tied to the reform and restructuring of the international economic order. There has been a lot of heat and smoke in the North-South dialogues; there is, however, very little light. It seems pretty dark even beyond the tunnel.

The Muslims feel dissatisfied with the whole developmental effort on all the above counts. They are further disturbed by the amoral character of the entire growth philosophy, which is steeped in the ethos of western culture and its secular liberalism. In the context of the Muslim societies this has acted as a centrifugal force, tearing the Muslim societies into warring nationalities, regions and classes. A totally materialistic approach is alien to the Islamic way of life and the historical tradition of the Muslim people. Islam wants to transform human society and restructure its socio-economic life according to the values of justice and fair play. It also seeks to weld the moral and material approaches into a unified and integrated approach to life and its problems. Any approach that splits life into secular and religious dimensions is anathema to Islam.

It is widely believed among Muslims that the western approach has been based on a disrespect, albeit not always explicitly articulated, for other cultures and social systems. As a result, efforts have been made to transplant western values and cultural patterns on to other peoples, leading to the disintegration of their cultures. This has been justified as imperatives of the process of modernisation. All this has been systematised into a theory of change stipulating that values and institutions that favour and strengthen exclusively materialistic considerations, motives, incentives, results...are the prime movers of social systems. Competition and reward have been made to replace long sustained humanistic attitudes and customs. People's motivation patterns, valued social institutions, relationships and systems of pecuniary reward and punishment have had to change to suit the alleged demands of economic development. Even those who do not subscribe to the Rostowian stages of growth do accept the substance of his analysis of the nature and direction of social change.

The Muslims look upon the entire developmental exercise as a grotesque effort aimed at cultural imperialism. Their main objections may be summarised thus:

1. The West-inspired approach to material prosperity has promoted in Muslim society an imitative mentality which is inimical to creativity and destroys originality. This not only aggravates the trends towards moral decay in the society but also perpetuates the hegemony of western culture on Muslim lands. It promotes an active collusion between the West and the westernised elite in the Muslim

world because development of Third World countries as cultural satellites of the West is bound to ensure an ever-increasing demand for western products.

2. A systematic application of this development strategy has proved to be highly divisive in Muslim society, splitting it up into modern and traditional, liberal and conservative, urban and rural, rich and poor and so on. This has perpetuated colonial traditions and encouraged consumption habits that tear the modern sector from the rest of the society and tie it in with its counterparts in the western world. This has led to the enrichment of a privileged minority and the impoverishment of the mass of people. It has engendered economic and social dualism and new tensions and conflicts within society. Lifestyles are changing in such a way that a high consumption-oriented privileged society is being imposed upon a mass of people committed to a different set of values and traditions. This is alienating the allegedly developing sections of the society from the rest. Symbols of modernisation are becoming targets of hatred.

3. The entire experiment has been terribly wasteful and extremely costly. Import substitution has failed to enhance the real technological capabilities of the economy, yet it is making a large number of people addicted to new luxuries and lifestyles that the society cannot, and should not, afford. A high consumption society is being created in countries that have little to consume. The patterns of consumption and production have become distorted, and tilted to serve the whims and fancies of a privileged minority. The real gains to society have been minimal.

4. There has been a metamorphosis of attitudes in the direction of hedonistic individualism. Concern for individual standards of living has taken precedence over that of strengthening the economic base of the nation. Greed and corruption have raised their ugly heads.

5. At the root of this approach is the assumption that an economic system can move on its own without simultaneous deliberate changes in political system, social institutions and moral attitudes of the people. It is assumed that the delicate balance that exists between different aspects of individual and social life will readjust itself in

the light of the changed economic situation. The experience, on the other hand, is that this has divided the society and added to friction, rivalry, confusion and waste.

Consequently, Muslim scholars preach that the totality and integrity of the social system has been ignored. This is at variance with the Islamic approach which stands for a happy balance between different aspects of life and aims at the development of an integrated personality in the individual and a happy balance in society.

They proclaim that such an imitative and exclusively materialistic strategy of economic development is repugnant to Islam, which is not a religion in the limited sense of the word, but has its own socio-economic programme based on its own world view and a set of ethical values and principles. Historical evidence indicates that the efforts to transplant western values and culture are proving counter-productive. Modernisation experiments have only touched the fringe of the *Ummah* and have failed to take root in its mainstream. This approach has been superficial, as it has sought for artificial change, which is bound to prove abortive. A number of western developmental institutions have failed to become an integral part of the society on which they have been transplanted.

Moreover, the conditions in which development took place in the West in the 18th and 19th centuries and the conditions, which prevail in contemporary Muslim societies, are very different. It is naive to assume that what worked in the West at a particular moment in history will equally work anywhere. Again, there is reaction against many of the modernisation ideals of the West within the West, particularly among its younger generations, which are increasingly attracted to what has been described as "counter-culture". The scenario is changing and today's Muslims, particularly young people, are discouraged to perpetuate what the revivalists deem as instruments and symbols of western dominance. The Muslim mind is demanded to realise the tricky chess game and rather than wasting time on useless pursuits, it must crave for the evolution of a new development strategy.

A Theological Insight into the Islamic Economy

To the Muslims, the economy is not left unattended by Islam. It is an inseparable part of the Islamic life and accordingly it must receive due attention. Despite the strategic significance of the economy, Muslims deem that this issue has been overlooked under political circumstances caused by Western colonialism. Although incomprehensive, Muslim thinkers have been able to produce accounts of what is meant by the Islamic economy. They argue that every system, intending to achieve certain goals, must be designed in a realistic manner. Therefore, if the system is supposed to be implemented in order to serve human life, particularly in the long-run, it must serve man's goals and be consistent with his *fitrah* (primordial nature). This is not possible unless the designer of the system has a command over the knowledge necessary for understanding social and individual aspects of man. Besides, the designer should have a thorough understanding of actual relations between those two aspects of man and the primordial nature of man as well. In addition to these prerequisites, the designer should understand the historical trends of such a relationship, the needs for development of such relationships and methods for pursuing those needs in order to realise an evolutionary, human approach toward realising the goals of the creation of man.

Indeed, the way the aforesaid satisfaction of needs is to be carried out should not overlap other systems which are meant to fulfill other needs of man. In other words, such a system should observe a wise balance and study the role and interrelationship of other systems which together comprise the whole system of life.

If we assume that the designer of the system possesses all those necessary prerequisites, we should assess subsequent stages in the process of achieving the desirable realism which is necessary for a system to be able to provide a proper context for itself. By this we mean the extent to which this system is compatible with the norms and values of the society (where the system is to be implemented), the extent of consistence between those norms and values and the emotional values presented by the system, and finally the extent to which this system assures the realisation of a desirable education to create social obedience for those ideological views and emotional values.

Although the system may be realistic, accurate, and rational in perceiving the reality and understanding its needs and their satisfaction, it will remain incapable if it is not preceded by an ideological impetus which supplies the society with bases for the stance that it should take toward the universe, life, and man itself. Consequently, the ideological impetus will guarantee the system the element of *iman* (faith). This element releases the system from the most important civilizational maladies including *ilhad* (atheism), which is the opposite of *iman*, and *shirk* (polytheism), which signifies the excessive belief in false gods, and *shakk* (doubt), which is in a manner resembling other destructive attitudes. Unless these requirements are realised, we cannot assure the provision of the first contextual element for the system's implementation. Similarly, as long as emotional motivations, which are the focus of education, are not perfectly compatible and harmonious with the ideological structure of the society, we cannot guarantee balance in man's personality when there is a wide gap between his beliefs and the internal and external values and motivations that the system provides in order to satisfy his needs. Moreover, these emotional motivations cannot form human behaviour and action unless they are strong and clearly defined.

By the above introduction to the main issue, Muslim scholars intend to indicate the necessity of two factors for every system intended to materialise its human goals: first, the planner's holistic approach towards human reality, including his relations and needs as well as their fulfilment concomitant with the rest of the system; second, facilitating its implementation through faith and compatible emotional motivations.

The Muslim theologians (*Ahlul Kalam*) argue that philosophically realism, in turn, requires the following two fundamental factors: first, the system should contain legal guarantees binding all those who oppose the harmonious human nature or those few who have not chosen the complete *iman* or the full commitment to the requirements of *iman*; second, it has a perfect flexibility to accommodate the temporal and spatial variations in human life and provides fixed solutions for fixed elements of human life and flexible ones for the accommodation of its alterable elements.

The prevailing belief in the Islamic world is that Islam was correct in announcing its rule in the form of general rules. Thus, it did not ignore any one of those aspects, but observed them perfectly and completed the religion which provides appropriate answers to man's needs till the Day of Judgement.

Accordingly, it announces that the whole Islamic system is based on reality and nature and that it is the fixed truth aiming at serving human beings and accomplishing the purpose of His creation. Thus, it enjoins whatever is desirable and forbids whatever is refused by nature.

They quote verses from Quran which, they believe, support above conception, verses such as:

'Then set your face upright for religion in the right state, the nature made by Allah in which He has made men. There is no alteration in Allah's creation. That is the right religion but most people do not know.' (30:30)

"Say: O people! Indeed there has come to you the truth from your Lord..." (10:108)

"O you who believe! Answer (the call of) Allah and the Apostle when he calls you to that which gives you life, and know that Allah intervenes between man and his heart, and that to Him you shall be gathered." (8:24)

"Those who follow the Apostle Prophet, who was taught neither to read nor to write, whom they find written down with them in the *Tawrah* and the *Injil* (Old and New Testaments), (who) enjoins them to do good and forbids them from doing evil, and makes the pure and good things *halal* (lawful) for them and makes impure and harmful things *haram* (prohibited) for them, and remove from them their burden and the shackles which were upon them. So (as for) those who believe in him and support him and help him and follow the light which was sent down with him, they are indeed the saved." (7:157)

The proof of this argument is the same proof that is quoted in the Islamic theology and substantiates for the Creator omniscience as well as the full and absolute control over the formation of shari'ah (the comprehensive body of Islamic rules).

There are numerous Quranic verses which are understood as perfect evidence in God's omniscience and duly His absolute entitlement to be recognised as the perfect designer of all systems required for man's life. On the other hand God is described frequently as the most beneficent, the most merciful which in turn implies He would apply the best systems conceivable to facilitate human life. The Quran says:

"Does He not know Who He created? He is Who made the earth smooth for you, therefore go about in the spacious sides thereof, and eat of His sustenance, and to Him is the return after death." (67:14-15)

"Say: Allah suffices as a witness between me and you. Surely He is Aware of His servants, and Seeing. And whomsoever Allah guides, is the follower of the right way, and whomsoever He causes to err, you shall not find for him guardians besides Him. And We will gather them together on the day of resurrection on their faces, blind and dumb and deaf. Their abode is hell, whenever it becomes allayed We will add to their burning." (17:96-97)

The above arguments and words with more or less various detailed approaches are usually used to prepare for discussions which touch the core of the matter. The *ulema* often takes the following points in their presentations of the Islamic economy.

1. Major attributes of the Islamic economy, their natural character, and Islam's emphasis on them.
2. The proper grounds Islam prepares for its economic system.
3. Relationship between this system and other systems.
4. Flexibility of the Islamic economic system.

In the study of Islamic economy as a way which Islam prescribes for individual and social behaviour in the economic field and examines Islam's rules in this area, almost all Muslims conclude that its most important attribute is social justice. In this respect, they believe that Islamic economy resembles all other systems that claim to be serving the human being and realising his social aspirations but it differs from them in the details of its conception of social justice.

It is argued that justice cannot be realised unless the following requirements are met: first, believing in the private and social sectors on an equal and advanced level in a way that the private sector acts on the fulfilment of man's natural demands for possessing the result of his effort and obtaining the benefits of his business. While the public sector aims at guaranteeing that social action enjoys a social product through which the provision of some needs and shortages would become possible.

Second, faith in individual economic freedom as a general, continuous, comprehensive principle which stems from the nature of ownership along with the belief in the existence of some limits at which this freedom ends.

Third, faith in the principle of mutual responsibility. Islam guarantees, for every individual in Islamic society, subsistence level, i.e., provision of his natural needs. The government is obliged to provide this minimum for all and it is absolutely impermissible that even a single needy person is found in Islamic society. As regards to procedures needed to achieve this purpose a number of suggestions are at hand.

1. Obliging individuals to accomplish their responsibilities and duties with respect to the provision of the necessary needs of others.

2. Utilising the legal power of *waliy al-amr* (head of the Islamic government) to determine the limits of public and economic legal domain (*saddu mantaqat al-mubahat*) and through providing the government with the desirable power.

3. Emphasis on public properties and *anfal* (properties with no particular owner/s) which are designated by the government as public properties that the government oversees and uses to achieve the above goal.

4. Enforcement of financial punishments and methods that are devised by Islam to transfer private properties to public ownership as with respect to *mawqufat* (endowments) or the lands of inhabitants who perished or the dead without heirs and so forth.

5. Constantly bearing in mind and prompting the disposition of Islamic legislation which aims at fortifying the social structure for the realisation of this mutual responsibility.

Fourth, belief in the principle of social balance and refusal of the class system in the Islamic society. It was known through the third point that the required minimum is to provide subsistence for all individuals. As far as the maximum is concerned, the following factors ought to be taken into account:

1. The proscription of *tabdhir* and *israf* (wasting and squandering) in all areas, therefore, an individual cannot possibly trespass to the line of *israf.*

2. The ban on every action that leads to misuse of particular properties, and of *lahw* (amusement) and *mujun* (impudence).

3. The nullification of all social and economic privileges and stratification which discriminate between different groups of people.

Muslims emphasise that if one goes back and scrutinises all these features and also closely studies human nature and conscience one will find these features as principles that can be reached via secular analysis. This explains the return of each of the two extremist systems of capitalism and socialism to a moderate position after its collision with opposing natural factors as they believe.

The claim that these features can be concluded even through healthy course of secular thinking, to the Muslims, are even verifiable by the Islamic sacred scriptures. Two examples of the texts frequently quoted in this context are as follows:

The Quran says: "And the man shall gain nothing but what he strives for." (53:39) (naturally if we interpret it as including worldly possession).

It is related that Ali said: "This property is indeed neither mine nor yours but it is a collective property of the Muslims...what is earned by their hands does not belong to any mouths other than theirs."

There are some texts that emphasise economic freedom in a natural form, the most explicit of which is the rule on which all *fuqaha'* (Islamic scholars) rely, namely the rule *Al-nasu musallatuna 'ala amwalihim* (people are in control of their properties)). Naturally, there are some limits to this freedom which are mentioned by other *nusus* (texts) stressing that this restriction is only for the benefit of the individual and the society.

There are also texts that emphasise the inherence of mutual responsibility and co-operation and further consider all kinds of negligence with respect to this principle as a general rejection of *din* (faith and religion). Quran, for example, says: "Have you seen the person who rejects the religion? He is the one who treats the orphan with harshness, and does not urge (others) to feed the poor." (107:1-3)

To support the aforesaid conception there is also another group of texts which stress the necessity for the realisation of balance in society through prohibition of *israf* (financial prodigality) and also renunciation of poverty and providing subsistence for every individual.

Grounds for Culmination of the Islamic Economy

It is strongly believed in Islamic circles of the learned that there exists huge wealth of holy scriptures containing various concepts and numerous rules and that there are fixed historical laws which serve in their totality the cause of Islamic economy and prepare for the realisation of its far-reaching goals. A number of the main issues raised in these scriptures are as follows:

1. The Real ownership belongs to Allah. This principle is the most important tenet with its visible marks on the economic behaviour of Muslim individuals. Ownership belongs only to the Unpaired, Almighty Allah and He the Exalted bestowed an assumed, legal ownership upon the human being so that it distributes the properties among its individuals and exercises this ownership according to the purposes that Allah chose for the benefit of

humanity. This notion has great influence on the exclusion of negative effects of ownership in its absolute capitalistic form.

2. Ethical concepts in the service of economic cause: Islamic texts are held to include an ethical plan which contributes to the economic system of Islam and help to actualize its goals. Most of the *riwayat* (traditions), on one hand, encourage in the human being the spirit of co-operation, responsibility, Islamic fraternity, *ithar* (self-sacrifice), *zuhd* (piety), and compassion for the miseries and disadvantages of others. On the other hand, they drive away from the human being such vices as stinginess, greed, exclusivism, transgressing the rights of others, opportunism, avarice, and envy. It is widely opined that Islam's arguments on ethical and educational systems are based on uplifting the spirit of generosity in human beings placing this end before economic freedom and the possibility of using it to his own particular benefits.

3. *Al-infaq al-mustahabb* (commendable spending for a divine cause) and the extended life. This is said to be an operative solution to the problem of conflict between the inherent instincts for serving one's self and the desire for serving society. According to this notion, one begins with the prolongation of his own life and ends up with a level of eternity in the hereafter. He finds out that self-interest and social interest are integrated; a notion that encourages him to make continuous *infaq* (religious donation) which does not ever run out of its driving forces according to the principle which says "whoever establishes a favourable habit he will be rewarded both for it and for the action of whoever follows it." Within the same context it is emphatically reminded that the extended effect of *waqf* (transfer of ownership) since, as the result of these motivations, private property is transferred to public ownership and man's permanent exploitation of his property is realised.

4. *Shukr al-ni'mah* (gratitude for a blessing) means to make the best use of wealth, avoiding waste; so many Muslim *ulema* say that the major problem in the global economic domain does not lie in the weakness of growth rates of natural resources and their failure to keep up with population growth but in the failure to make ideal use of natural resources or, as the scriptures put it, in *kufran al-ni'mah* (ingratitude for the blessing) and squandering

the natural, mineral and animal resources and so forth. In this connection they qoute this Quranic verse:

"And He gave you of whatever you asked Him for and if you count Allah's blessings you will not (possibly) obtain their number. Man is indeed very unjust, very ungrateful..." (14:34))

And a category of *shukr al-ni'mah* would be to make ideal use of the labour force and to avoid wasting it. For this reason, the texts count the merits of working diligently and even make it obligatory for those who are capable of doing this kind of work.

5. Relationship between moralities and material pursuits at the cosmological level. Muslim theologians establish a cosmological link between the two and believe that nobody can perceive this link unless he believes in the *ghayb* (the metaphysical world) and its various aspects. The Holy Qur'an stresses that *zulm* (injustice) leads to *halak* (annihilation) saying "Thus, because of their injustice We destroyed them" and that *adl* (justice) and *du'a'* (praying) and *shukr* (gratitude) leads, in a lawful way, to *rakha'* (comfort), "Ask for your Lord's forgiveness, surely He is the most Forgiving, He will send down the cloud upon you pouring down abundance of rain. And help you with properties and sons, and make for you gardens and make for you rivers." (71:10-12). To these theologians this fact raises a great hope in the future, even the material future, and opens the way for social and economic dynamism.

The Economy in Conformity with Other Islamic Systems

It is a common conviction among Muslims that all systems devised by Islam are integral to each other and cover in their totality the whole universe. These systems are in strong and close interconnection in such a manner that none of them can achieve its desired goal without the other systems operating properly. In this regard the following points are usually discussed:

1. Certain areas of the social system are reserved to be supervised by the *valy al-amr* (the leader of the society) or by some one appointed by him due to his *ijtihad* (ability to extract Islamic rule whenever needed) and determination of the nature of the prevailing

situations and the *ummah's* interest. This is applicable, for example, in economic, legal, and penal systems and in the institutions of *waqf* (endowment), *mu'amalat* (transactions), *irth* (inheritance), and so forth. This fact indicates the complete connection between these institutions and the ruling political system.

2. The economic system is strongly related to the system of *'ibadat* (acts of worship). This is the issue which is sometimes presented in association with the prayers and zakah in tens of Qur'anic verses. *Zakah* (almsgiving) is a financial act of worship. Financial *kaffarat* (expiations) are, in fact, also a huge economic participation by *'ibadat* system in the service of public economic interest. It should not be ignored that some acts of worship like *sawm* (fasting) and *hajj* provide the elements of economic grounds. There are certain acts of worship that strongly contribute to the public ownership such as *waqf*, if we require *niyyat al-qurbah* (proximity intention) in it.

3. The economic system and its goals and peculiarities naturally have a strong connection with the system of *mu'amalat* (financial transactions). The Muslims believe Islam has designed this system in such a manner so as to provide the proper environment for the realisation of mutual responsibility, balance, and dual ownership, emphasise the labour element, and prohibits *riba* (usury), *'akl al-mali bi al-batil* (financial misappropriation), harmful acts, *lahw* (debauchery), and wasting of wealth.

4. There is a considerable linkage between the economic system and the system of jihad (military defence) in Islam for the latter system involves, in addition to combative rules and methods, implications for ownership, war spoils, and so forth.

5. Undoubtedly, the economic system is also related to the social system including the form of society's principle cell, i.e., the family, and also social relations among the families, and individual's relations with society. All of these are considered to be predominated by social Islamic rules including mutual responsibility and balance, which form the most important characteristics in the economy. This argument also involves the rules regarding *mahrs* (dowries), *nafaqahs* (allowances), various methods of division of labour, and such issues as *irth* (inheritance), *wasiiyyahs* (bequests), and the

rulings with regard to children, *qada'* (adjudication), financial *ta'zirs* (discretionary punishments) and other varieties of financial punishments, and so forth.

6. Mention was already made to the link held by Muslims between Islam's economic system and its ethical system which makes the latter one of the major preludes and motivating elements for the *ummah* in the way of implementing the economic system and realising its goals to such an extent that it becomes hard to distinguish between the two systems.

Resilience of the Islamic Economy

The fact that Islam puts forward certain broad economic rules and relates them to the *'urf* (prevailing standards of conduct) concept has a special connotation for notions like *israf* and *tabdhir* (wasting and squandering), *faqr* and *ghina* (poverty and needlessness), *al-nafaqat al-muta'arifah* (customary allowance), *al-manfa'at al-muhallalah* (lawful profit), *ma'un* (basic need), *riba* (usury), *mithliyyah* and *qimiyyah* (fundability and being ad valorem), circulation and depression of cash currencies, *damm* (liability), individual and social damage, *haraj* (impediment), *darurah* (urgency), *al-maslahat al-'ulya* (the higher expediency), being *asbaq* (preceding) in *waqf*, being *'aqdiy* (contractual), being *bay'iy* (exchange), trade through *taradi* (mutual agreement), being *qimariy* (gamble), *lahw*, and even *'adalah* (justice), *zulm* (injustice), *ta'addi* (transgression), and *akl al-mal bi al-batil* (misappropriation of property). Thus, *'urf* (common sense) intervenes when these concepts change, often due to change in conditions, and consequently, as a result of change in the *'urfi* view of the subject the judgement also changes.

However, the most important element on which the Islamic system concentrates is the element of intervention by the just *valiy al-amr* (the leader of *ummah*) in the economic life. In such a system, the *valiy* has the obligation to take advantage of his social power and true commitment to Islam and the Islamic expediency of the *ummah* and, through consultation with the masters of knowledge and expertise, carry out his duties which can be summarised as follows:

1. Identification of the best methods and executive arrangements for the enforcement of the fixed rules of Allah, e.g. looking for the best way to eliminate *riba* (usury) in society while preserving the positive activities performed by the banks.
2. Providing the public domain with laws in accordance with the supreme Islamic expediency while preserving, as much as possible, the prime directives regarding the various cases.
3. Determining the extent to which the conditions are favourable for the enforcement of Islamic rules and institutions.

Afghanistan's Economic Account

General Economic Data:
Gross National Product: USD $3,100,000,000 (1988).
Public Debt: USD $5,381,000,000 (1993).
Imports: USD $602,000,000 (1994).
Exports: USD $296,000,000 (1994).
Tourism Receipts: USD $1,000,000 (1998).
Balance of Trade: USD $-306,000,000,000 (1994).
Economically Active Population: 5,557,000 or 29.4% of total population (1994).
Main Trading Partners:
Afghanistan's main trading partners are the republics of the former USSR, the USA, Pakistan, Saudi Arabia and Germany.
Main Primary Products:
Barley, Coal, Copper, Cotton, Fruit, Goats, Iron, Maize, Natural Gas, Nuts, Rice, Sheep, Sugar, Vegetables, Wheat.
Major Industries:
Agriculture, Bicycles, Carpets, Cement, Food Processing, Footwear, Fur and Leather Products, Furniture, Plastics, Textiles.
Main Exports:
Carpets, Cotton, Fruit, Karakul Skins and Wool, Natural Gas, Nuts.

Economic Significance of Afghanistan at Ancient Times

A main offshoot of the Silk Road carrying luxury goods and ideas between Rome, India, and China passed through Afghanistan, where a transhipment centre existed at Balkh. Indian pilgrims travelling the Silk Road introduced Buddhism to China during the early centuries AD, and Buddhist art blossomed during this period. The world's largest Buddha figures (175 feet and 120 feet tall) were carved into a cliff at Bamian in the central mountains of Afghanistan during the 3rd and 4th centuries AD. Further evidence of trade and cultural achievement of the period has been recovered at the Kushan summer capital of Bagram, north of Kabul. This includes painted glass from Alexandria; plaster matrices, bronzes, porphyries, and alabasters from Rome; carved ivories from India; and lacquers from China. A massive Kushan city at Delbarjin, north of Balkh, and a major gold hoard of superb artistry near Sheberghan, west of Balkh, has also been excavated.

Afghanistan's Economic Resources

Extensive investigations have laid open the existence of a number of minerals of economic importance. The most important find has been that of natural gas, with considerable reservoirs near Sheberghan in Jowzjan province, near the Turkmen border, about 75 miles west of Mazar-e-Sharif. The Khvajeh Gugerdak and Yatim Taq fields are major producers, with storage and refining facilities. Pipelines deliver natural gas to Uzbekistan and Tajikistan and to a thermal power plant and chemical fertiliser plant in Mazar-e-Sharif. Petroleum wealth is considered to be insignificant. Many coal deposits have been found on the northern slopes of the Hindu Kush. Main coal fields are at Karkar and Eshposhteh, in Baghlan province, and Fort Sarkari, in Balkh province. High grade iron ore, with an iron content of 62-63 percent, has been discovered at Eajgak, 60 miles north west of Kabul. Copper is mined at Zaynak, near Kabul, and uranium is extracted in the mountains near Khvajeh Rawash, east of Kabul. There are also deposits of copper, lead, and zinc near

Konduz; beryllium in Khad Konak; chrome ore in the Lowgar valley near Herat; and the semiprecious stone lapis lazuli in Badakhshan. Afghanistan also has deposits of rock salt, beryl, barite, flour spar, bauxite, lithium, tantalum, gold, silver, asbestos, mica, and sulphur.

Afghanistan is essentially a pastoral country. Only 12 percent of the total land area is arable, and only about half of the arable acreage is cultivated annually. Much of the arable area consists of fallow cultivable land or steppes and mountains that serve as pasture land. In addition, a large area is desert. Forests cover about 3 percent of the total land area; they are found mainly in the eastern part of the country and on the southern slopes of the Hindu Kush. Those in the east consist mainly of conifers, providing timber for the building industry as well as some wild nuts for export. Other trees, especially oaks, are used as fuel. North of the Hindu Kush are pistachio trees, the nuts of which are exported.

Power Resources
Afghanistan is potentially rich in hydroelectric resources. However, the seasonal flow of the country's many streams and waterfalls— torrential in spring, when the snow melts in the mountains, but negligible in summer— necessitates the costly construction of dams and reservoirs in remote areas. The nation's inconsiderable demand for electricity renders such projects unprofitable except near large cities or industrial centres. The potential of hydroelectricity has been tapped substantially only in the Kabul-Jalalabad region.

The Economy of the Population
About two thirds of Afghanistan's people are farmers or herdsmen, but only about 12 percent of the land is cultivated. The remainder is either too rugged or too dry for farming. About 4 percent of the total land area is irrigated. Farmers use terrace, tunnel, and well methods to irrigate their land.

In the mid-1990s about half of Afghanistan's land area was being used for grazing. Afghanistan has vast herds of sheep, goats, cattle, horses, donkeys, and camels—as many as 20 million head. Of these, sheep number about 14 million; cattle, 1.5 million; and goats, 2 million. The sheep provide wool and skins for clothing and flesh for meat.

The farmers live in the fertile valleys or on the plain, wherever water is available for irrigation. Wheat, corn (maize), grapes, and rice are the chief crops. Industrial crops include cotton, sugar beet, and sugarcane. Oilseed, nuts, and fruits, particularly grapes, are also important, and large quantities of vegetables, especially potatoes, are grown. Agriculture contributes more than half of the gross domestic product.

Aided by loans and grants from the World Bank and other sources, Afghanistan's governments have tried since World War II to ameliorate economic circumstances.

The Helmand Valley project, undertaken with aid from the United States, was designed to supply water for 1,000 square miles (2,600 square kilometers) of desert. With aid from the former Soviet Union, the Afghan government built the Nangarhar Canal near Jalalabad in the south.

Afghanistan has little industry. By estimate, only about 20,000 persons make up the industrial labor force; most of them are employed in the cotton-textile industry. Others work in the cement, sugar, vegetable oil, woollen and artificial silk textile, and fruit-processing industries. Handworkers in cottage industries produce woven, embroidered, metal, pottery, and wooden goods and utensils. Cottage industries account for some 8 percent of the gross domestic product, while manufacturing industries account for only about 4 percent. The yearly income per person in Afghanistan was about 280 dollars in the mid-1990s.

Economic Administration until 1994

When Afghanistan began to draw up the development of its economy in the mid-1950s, it lacked not only the necessary social structure and institutions for modern economic activities but also managerial and technical skills. The country was at a much lower stage of economic development than most of its neighbours. Between 1956 and 1979, however, the country's economic growth was guided by several five-year and seven-year plans and was aided by extensive foreign assistance, primarily from the former Soviet Union and the United States. Roads, dams, power plants, and factories were constructed, irrigation projects carried out, and education broadened. The Soviet invasion in 1979 and the later civil war profoundly disordered Afghanistan's economic development. Agricultural production declined and food shortages were reported and, with the exception of natural gas production and some other industries considered essential by the Soviet Union, industrial production stagnated. Thus, Afghanistan remains economically one of the world's poorest countries.

The Socialist governments had announced their commitment to developing a mixed, guided economy by means of a series of five-year plans. In practice, the effectiveness of such a policy was limited by the insufficiency of government resources, by a cumbersome bureaucracy, and by a shortage in technical personnel. Before the Soviet invasion, the government budget was divided into two parts, ordinary and development. The former covered administrative activities and the latter investment expenditures, incorporated into the national plans of development. Total domestic revenue was usually exceeded by expenditures; the difference was covered through deficit financing and foreign loans and grants. Following the Soviet invasion, a balanced budget was achieved with revenue derived principally from the sale of natural gas and from foreign loans and grants. Expenditure was mainly for government ministries, the developmental budget, and foreign debt service. The private sector engaged primarily in agriculture and livestock breeding. There formerly existed a mixed pattern of small, medium, and large land holdings, but this system underwent drastic change, particularly after 1978. The bulk of the trade and transport and most manufacturing were in the hands of private entrepreneurs until the late 1970s when these sectors of the economy were nationalised. Public enterprise was formerly confined to a section of the foreign trade, to mining, and to some industries. Because most of the population was and still is engaged in agriculture, the industrial labour force is insignificant, and labour unions failed to develop. Another hindrance in economic plans of the governments was the fact that traditional loyalties to families and tribes were stronger than those to workers' organisations.

In 1975 the government nationalised all banks. The largest bank in the country, the Bank of Afghanistan, is the centre of the formal banking system. It is the sole bank of issue, and it plays an important role in determining and implementing the government's financial policies. There are private money traders who provide nearly all the services of a commercial bank.

Most of the foreign trade of Afghanistan was controlled by the government or by government-controlled monopolies. During the socialist era the USSR was the leading trading partner.

Taliban's Economic Agenda

Islamic Law contains general economic rules and regulations which require a good deal of study in order to respond to challenges and complexities of the modern world. This study, however, is not by any means an easy task. The experience of the Islamic states reveal that there have always been enigmas regarding clear cut Islamic rules concerning some issue of absolutely modern nature such as the banking system and its competitiveness locally and internationally.

The Taliban will not be immune to the disadvantages of launching an economic discovery voyage of their own. Although they have made it clear that at this stage their concentration is primarily focused on their military ends, they have to realise the integral roles of political and economic plans.

The Taliban administration insists, even in statements dealing with civil issues such as economy, that these issues are being handled within the framework provided by Islam. Concerning enhancement of the economy they insist on necessity of de-arming the people and subduing the opposition in order to achieve peace and an appropriate atmosphere for commercial transactions. Again to accomplish this mission they press for the need for execution of *Hudood-o-Qisas* and *ta'zirat* (Shara'ee code of punishment) to wipe out what they call vice and evil from society. On the other hand they consider practising the "golden" principles of Islam as a precondition to establishing a booming economy and to placing it on a strong and solid foundation. Taliban propagate their concern with economy from time to time through their media:

> Several steps have been taken to ensure the achievement of these aims. Ministers are working *Fi-Sabeelillah* without pay; and are not using government resources for private use; curtailing expenses, refraining from indulgence in squandering and extravagance, are all steps taken in this direction. Likewise, from time to time, suitable measures are also announced to improve agriculture, to reorganise and revive unproductive industrial units and to give vast concessions to businessmen for the promotion of trade activities.

Some members of the Supreme Shura (assembly) like Maulvi Saif-ud-deen Farooqi are specially delegated to attend to the business issues. They hold meetings with businessmen and help draw a wider plan for improving Taliban economy. In these meetings Mr Farooqi and his colleagues meet delegations or individuals of Afghan businessmen. These meetings are usually prearranged and their purpose is to boost trade and industry within the Taliban domain. These meetings sometimes result in the formation of embryonic creations such as a Shura to undertake work for "improving and modernising agriculture, for the revival of industrial activities and enforcement of measures taken to facilitate businessmen in the promotion of trade activities."

In some of these meetings messages from the Taliban leader are read out in which he encourages and urges the Afghan businessmen and traders to work with the government in reconstructing the war-ravaged country. In a meeting which was followed by announcement of the aforesaid *Shura*, Mulla Umar the leader of Taliban, in a part of his message said:

"...eighteen years of war had ruined the economy, therefore the world businessmen in general, and the Afghan businessmen in particular, should invest in Afghanistan. He further added that the first priority for Afghan businessmen should be the regular supply of foodstuffs."

These meetings at which issues of economic importance are discussed are supplemented by efforts made by the ministry of finance headed by Maulvi Ehsan-ullah Ehsan. Promotion of foreign investment in Afghanistan seems to be the only option which brings desperately needed funds to feed new projects and revive unfinished ones.

Drug Business and Taliban Economy

Poppy cultivation and opium and heroin production have reportedly skyrocketed in Afghanistan since the Taliban movement extended its control across most of the country, according to US anti-drug experts and international relief organisations.

The US and international drug experts estimate that Afghanistan is the second-largest opium producer in the world and that it is responsible for the production of more than one-third of the world's opium and heroin, which is refined from opium. The same sources say that the Taliban control 96 percent of Afghanistan's poppy growing regions and reap profits by taxing poppy growers and those who refine poppies into opium.

According to a statement released by the US State Department in March as the Taliban expanded their control over Afghanistan's opium-growing territory, they appear to have expanded their drug involvement as well, including facilitating major traffickers to move large quantities of morphine base and heroin to the West.

"The Taliban tax opium, they tax morphine, and they levy fees on transport." They reap tens of millions of dollars a year from the drug trade, even though they initially said they were against it," US sources claimed.

The Taliban's claimed involvement in the drug trade would seem to conflict with the strict rules it has imposed on Afghans in keeping with its interpretation of Islam. Taliban leaders have denied any connection with drug trafficking and have maintained that they will eradicate opium poppy crops once they have established order in the fractious country and can persuade poppy growers that they can grow other crops profitably.

Besides causing tension with the West, the increase in drug trafficking involving Afghanistan is a growing irritant for neighbouring Iran, which opposed the Taliban's take-over of Afghanistan. At a September 1997 conference of the international policing agency Interpol, the Iranian representative directly accused the Taliban of being "the main source of the death trade," according to a source with direct knowledge of the event.

US officials said that as Iran has softened its stance toward the West, it has begun to take drug interdiction more seriously. Iran has made so much progress, these officials say, that in a presidential announcement Iran received US government certification as a nation that is fighting drug trafficking. Since the annual certification process was initiated in 1986, Iran had never been given the stamp of US approval. Afghanistan also has routinely failed to obtain certification.

The US State Department report said poppy production had increased dramatically in Qandahar province, which is both the heartland of the Taliban movement and the base of operations for Osama bin Laden, the radical Saudi exile whom US officials accused of running one of the largest terrorist networks in the world.

Grounds for Western Investment in Afghanistan

As regards their tough political attitudes towards issues of sensitivity to the Western world, the Taliban are expected to represent a serious threat in regional flux of commerce. However, they are well informed that business with the outside world is and must be considered the main task of their administration. In a previous chapter an analogy was offered concerning resemblances of the Taliban with Ibn Saud's political progress in Saudi Arabia. In Ibn Saud's experience the danger of Islamic fanaticism manifested itself when he was just about to launch his political and economic reforms.

His incorporation of new technology was called innovation and his ties with the western powers were described as alliance with *Kuffar* (disbelievers). Ibn Saud soon realised he could not get on with his development plans unless he was released from fanatic pressures. Although these fanatics represented by Ikhwan hard-liners had fought in Ibn Saud's army, however the clash of views brought them face to face with him on the battle front. The confrontation ended with Ibn Saud's victory and the economic as well as political plans continued as scheduled by the King. The Taliban leadership is fully aware of the presence of strong opposition to normalisation of ties with the West irrespective of political and economic necessities. This is not a surprise since the whole philosophy of the Taliban emergence and their antipathy against other Islamic groups are based on it. Nevertheless the relaxed attitude of Taliban in their contacts with foreign powers and international companies contain an element of flexibility. They have frequently made clear that they have no reservations whatsoever as regards foreign investments in Afghanistan. In a way they are different from their neighbouring Muslim fundamentalists in Iran whose unclear stand towards international commercial law has caused them irreparable damage to this day. *Dharb-i-Mu'min* reported a message sent by Mulla Umar to a meeting held between some Taliban authorities and influential businessmen. The paper reported:

> *Ameer al-Mu'mineen* (commander of the faithful) urged the Afghan businessmen and traders to work with the government in reconstructing the war-ravaged country. He said that eighteen years of war had ruined the economy, therefore the world businessmen in general, and Afghan businessmen in particular, should invest in Afghanistan. He further added that the first priority for Afghan businessmen should be the regular supply of foodstuffs. In the meeting, Haji Shah Wali, the president of the trade union told the Minister about the difficulties and hurdles faced by Afghan businessmen. Similarly, a group of businessmen from Herat, met with the Finance Minister, Maulvi Ehsan-ullah Ehsan and told him about their troubles. The Finance Minister, while assuring them of his full co-operation, stressed on them to make full use of the co-operation of the government, because strengthening of the Taliban will be the

strengthening of such a system which will guarantee the betterment of people belonging to different walks of life.

The report also reported a meeting of Afghan businessmen with the Interior Minister, Mulla Khairullah Khairkhwah. The Minister stressed on the need for concrete measures to overcome ills plaguing the economy. *Dha'rb-i Mu'min* also printed the statement of the Afghan Ambassador, Mufti Ma'soom Afghani, in its Urdu issue, in which the ambassador has urged Pakistani businessmen and business community to invest in Afghanistan instead of Central Asian Republics (CIRs) and the opening of the Torkhum border is a step in this direction. He added "the steps taken by the Taliban Government for economic reform will have beneficial effects on the people and trading communities of Afghanistan and Pakistan."

Afghanistan's Natural Resources

Since ancient times, deposits of gold, silver, copper, beryl, and lapis lazuli have been mined in small quantities in the mountainous areas. Salt has been mined in increasing quantities, and production now meets the needs of the country. Coal deposits have been exploited, and production rose to an estimated 167,000 metric tons per year in 1987. Large natural-gas deposits in northern Afghanistan were developed with Soviet financing. Gas began flowing to the USSR in the mid-1970s. Other deposits, such as iron ore, sulphur, chrome, zinc, and uranium, are still largely unexploited.

Historical Oil and Gas Survey

The Soviets had estimated Afghanistan's proven and probable natural gas reserves at up to 5 trillion cubic feet. Afghan gas production reached 275 million cubic feet per day in the mid-1970s. However, due to declining reserves from producing fields, output gradually fell to about 220 Mmcf/d by 1980. At that time, the Djarquduq field was brought online and was expected to boost

Afghan gas output to 385 Mmcf/d by the early 1980s. However, sabotage of infrastructure by the anti-Soviet Mujahideen restricted the country's total production to 290 Mmcf/d, an output level which was held fairly steady until the Soviet withdrawal in 1989. After the Soviet withdrawal and subsequent Afghan civil war, roughly 31 producing wells at Shibrigan area fields were shut pending the restart of gas sales to the former Soviet Union.

At its height in the late 1970s, Afghanistan supplied 70%-90% of its natural gas production to the Soviet Union's gas grid via a link through Kushka, Turkmenistan. In 1992, Afghan President Najibullah indicated that a new gas sales agreement with Russia was in progress. However, several former Soviet republics raised price and distribution issues and negotiations stalled. In the early 1990s, Afghanistan also discussed possible gas supply arrangements with Hungary, Czechoslovakia, and several Western European countries, but these talks never progressed further. In 1996, Afghan gas production was around 19 Mmcf/d, all of which was used domestically.

Soviet estimates from the late 1970s placed Afghanistan's proven and probable oil and condensate reserves at 95 million barrels. Despite plans to start commercial oil production in Afghanistan, all oil exploration and development work as well as plans to build a 10,000 barrel per day refinery were halted after the 1979 Soviet invasion. Afghanistan's various provinces receive refined products from neighbouring countries. In August 1996, the Pakistani government agreed to transport an undisclosed amount of oil products to Kabul.

Energy Sector under the Taliban

As of late August 1998, following a series of military victories, the Taliban had gained control of approximately 90 per cent of Afghanistan (including the capital, Kabul, captured in October 1996). According to news reports by Dow Jones and other sources, Taliban military victories included the capture of various territories, including: 1) the northern stronghold of Uzbek warlord Rashid

Dostum; 2) the city of Mazar-e-Sharif; 3) Taloqan, the capital of Takhar province; and 4) Hayratan, Pul-e-Kumrl and Doshi. These conquests leave only three isolated pockets of resistance to the Taliban in Afghanistan: the central Hazara territory around Bamiyan; the mountainous north eastern provinces around Badakhshan; and the Panjshir Valley.

Afghanistan's significance from an energy standpoint stems from its geographical position as a potential transit route for oil and natural gas exports from Central Asia to the Arabian Sea. A multinational consortium led by US-based Unocal has proposed building multi-billion dollar oil and gas export pipelines through Afghanistan, although these plans have now been thrown into serious question. In February 1998, the Taliban announced plans to revive the Afghan National Oil Company, which was abolished by the Soviet Union after it invaded Afghanistan in 1979. The company is expected to play an important role in the resumption of oil and gas exploration in Afghanistan.

In January 1998, the Taliban signed an agreement that would allow a proposed 890-mile, $2-billion, 2-billion-cubic-feet-per-day natural gas pipeline project led by Unocal to proceed. Unocal subsequently estimated that construction on the line, which would transport gas from Turkmenistan's 45-Tcf Dauletabad gas field to Pakistan, would begin in late 1998. The proposed $2-billion pipeline would tentatively run from Dauletabad south to the Afghan border and through Herat and Qandahar in Afghanistan, to Quetta, Pakistan. The line would then link with Pakistan's gas grid at Sui. Gas shipments had been projected to start at 700 Mmcf/d in 1999 and to rise to 1.4 Bcf/d or higher by 2002. In March 1998, however, Unocal announced a delay in finalising project details due to Afghanistan's continuing civil war. In June 1998, Gazprom announced that it was relinquishing its 10 per cent stake in the gas pipeline project consortium (known as the Central Asian Gas Pipeline Ltd., or Centgas), which was formed in August 1996. Unocal and Saudi Arabia's Delta Oil hold a combined 85 per cent stake in the consortium, while Turkmenrusgas owns 5 per cent. Other participants in the project include Hyundai Engineering &

Construction Company of South Korea, Itochu Corporation of Japan, and Indonesia Petroleum Ltd.

In August 1998, Unocal announced that it was suspending its role in the Afghanistan gas pipeline project in light of the recent US government military action in Afghanistan, and also due to intensified fighting between the Taliban and opposition groups. Unocal has stressed that the gas pipeline project will not proceed until an internationally recognised government is in place. To date, only three countries—Saudi Arabia, Pakistan and the United Arab Emirates—have recognised the Taliban government.

Besides the gas pipeline, Unocal has also considered building a 1,000-mile, 1-million barrel-per-day capacity oil pipeline that would link Chardzou, Turkmenistan to Pakistan's Arabian Sea Coast via Afghanistan. Since the Chardzou refinery is already linked to Russia's Western Siberian oil fields, this line could provide a possible alternative export route for regional oil production from the Caspian Sea. The $2.5 billion pipeline is known as the Central Asian Oil Pipeline Project. For a variety of reasons, including high political risk and security concerns, however, financing for this project remains highly questionable.

Despite a wealthy variety of extensive mineral deposits, transportation difficulties, war, and lack of native technical skills and equipment has hindered full exploitation of such resources. Much natural gas is located in the north which is rather mountainous.

Climate

Climatic conditions in Afghanistan exhibit great daily and seasonal variations, largely because of the extremes in elevation that characterise the country. During the day, variations in temperature may range from freezing conditions at dawn to almost 38° C (100° F) at noon. Summer temperatures as high as 49° C (120° F) have been recorded in the northern valleys. Midwinter temperatures as low as -9.4° C (15° F) are common at the 1980-m (6500-ft) level in the Hindu Kush. Kabul, situated at an elevation of about 1830 m (about 6000 ft), has cold winters and pleasant summers. Jalalabad (about 550 m/about 1800 ft high) is subtropical, and the climate of Kandahar (about 1070 m/about 3500 ft high) is mild. Afghanistan is a relatively dry country, the annual rainfall averaging about 305 mm (about 12 in). Most of the rainfall occurs between October and April. Sandstorms occur frequently in the deserts and arid plains.

Transportation

Afghanistan is a predominantly mountainous country; about three-fourth of its surface consists of uplands. The main lowlands are a series of river valleys in the north and various desert regions in the south and south west. The principal mountain system of the country is the Hindu Kush, which, with its various offshoots, extends for about 965 km (about 600 mls.) from the Pamirs, a range in the north east, to the borders of Iran in the west. The average altitude of the Hindu Kush is about 4270 m (about 14,000 ft); some peaks are about 7620 m (about 25,000 ft) high. Natural passes penetrate the mountains of Afghanistan at various points, facilitating travel within the nation as well as communication with neighbouring countries. In the Hindu Kush the only pass lower than 3050 m (10,000 ft) is the Shibar (2987m/9800 ft), which connects the Kabul region with the northern part of the country. Probably the best known of the mountain passes is the historic Khyber Pass on the north eastern border, which traverses the Sulaiman Range and affords relatively easy access to Pakistan.

Communications

The state-controlled telephone and telegraph lines serve all principal cities and smaller towns as well. Telegraphic communications exist among the major cities and between Kabul and Peshawar. In the mid-1980s about 32,000 telephones were in use.

Six newspapers appeared regularly in the late 1980s. The government broadcasting network serves about 150,000 radios and 20,000 television receivers.

6

Social Order and Human Rights under the Taliban

Taliban and Education

Taliban religious militia shut down more than 100 private schools on June 16, 1998. These schools were educating thousands of girls in defiance of the Taliban's ban on education for girls.

The Taliban Minister in charge Haji Khulimuddin announced the closure at a news conference in the capital, Kabul. He warned that violators would be punished. The Taliban had permitted the schools to function without officially recognizing them. According to estimates provided in January by several international aid groups, at least 107 so-called informal schools in Kabul were providing education to more than 6,500 children, half of whom were girls.

When the Taliban militia swept into Kabul in September 1996, it shut down girls' schools, claiming the curriculum was against the tenets of Islam. Schools for boys have since reopened, and the Taliban has allowed girls, 8 and younger, to study only the Islamic holy book, the Quran. After the age of 8, girls must leave school.

Mr Khulimuddin told reporters that the Taliban discovered several 14 and 15-year-old girls receiving education in private homes. "These schools weren't just for children. They also included 14 and 15-year-old girls," he said. "These schools were operating against the principles of Islamic law."

The Taliban also announced it was shutting down vocational training programs for girls. This will effectively shut down dozens of programs, such as carpet weaving and sewing projects, that have been quietly running to give young girls a skill and a way to earn money.

The Taliban minister mentioned above also accused foreign aid workers associated with these home schools for propagating anti-Taliban propaganda.

Khulimuddin said school operators will have to apply for a license from the Ministry of Education before they are allowed to operate.

"Right now, we have no control over these schools," he said. "If they get permission, then we can control them."

It seems that the academic system in Afghanistan under the Taliban may not be capable of producing a sufficient number of the qualified graduates needed in construction projects for quite some time. Having mentioned that one must take note of the fact that even in pre-Taliban Afghanistan for a variety of reasons the academic arena did not accomplish sufficient progress quantitatively and qualitatively.

Although elementary schooling was free and compulsory for children aged 7 through 15, only about 25 percent of the people aged 15 or more years were literate. In the late 1980s, elementary and secondary schools had an annual enrollment of more than 700,000 students. Institutions of higher education had an enrollment of some 10,000 students.

The Taliban have repeatedly assured that these closures are temporary and will last until they find an Islamically appropriate system. However this would be an extremely demanding task which requires tremendous resources both intellectually and materially. One must also note that this practice of the Taliban is not without precedent.

One of the first measures adopted by the Iranian government after the Revolution in 1979 was the desecularization of the public schools system. This was a three-pronged program that involved purging courses and textbooks believed to slander Islam and substituting courses on religion; purging teachers to ensure that only those who understood the true meaning of Islam (i.e., were not secular) remained in the schools; and regulating the behavior and dress of students.

Although the government reintroduced the study of religion into the public school curriculum from primary grades through college, it did not act to alter the basic organization of the education system. Thus, as late as the school year 1986-1987, schools had not changed significantly from the pattern prior to the Revolution. Students studied in primary schools for five years, beginning the first grade at about age seven. Then they spent three years, designated the guidance cycle, in a middle school. In this cycle, the future training of students was determined by their aptitude as demonstrated on examinations. Students were then directed into one of three kinds of four-year high schools: the academic cycle, preparing for college; the science and mathematics cycle, preparing for university programs in engineering and medicine; and the vocational technical cycle.

The Ministry of Education announced that nearly 11.5 million students were registered for elementary and secondary schools during the academic year 1986-1987. Statistics on the percentage of young people aged seven through nineteen enrolled in school have not been available since the Revolution. It is generally estimated that the percentages have remained similar to those before the Revolution: school attendance of about 78 percent of elementary-age children and less than 50 percent of secondary-age youth.

Since the Revolution, higher education in Iran experienced significantly more drastic changes than elementary and secondary education. The university campuses became centers of conflict between students who supported a thorough desecularization of administrations, faculties, and curricula and students who wanted to retain a secular system. There were violent clashes at several universities in the 1979-1980 school year; as a result the government closed all 200 institutes of higher learning in April 1980. The universities were then purged of professors and students considered insufficiently Islamic and were not completely reopened until the fall of 1983. When the colleges resumed classes, they enrolled only a fraction of the 1979 to 1980 student body. At the University of Tehran, Iran's largest, student enrollment was reduced from 17,000 to 4,500; similarly large declines were registered at other institutions. The decline in the number of female students was even more dramatic: whereas on the eve of the revolution women had constituted about 40 percent of the total number of students in higher education, after 1983 they formed only 10 percent.

Back to Afghanistan, the Taliban have indicated they are willing to promote an independent academic system of their own. However their statements dealing with educational systems are mostly made in general terms and cannot be fully expressive of a profoundly meditated plan. For instance, in a communication broadcast by the Taliban media, minister of information and member of the Supreme Shura, Mulla Ameer Khan Muttaqi informed Al-Rasheed Trust (a trust with its headquarters in Pakistan) on behalf of the Ministry of Education that "in accordance with the directives of *Ameer-ul-M'umineen*, new universities and colleges are being opened to provide higher education to ten thousand students in each province of Kandhar, Kabul, Herat and Jalalabad, and new Madaris are being established for five hundred students in each of the other eighteen provinces. Al-Rasheed Trust should now come forward to assist in the completion of this noble, purely religious work." This announcement contained elements of what the Taliban have in mind concerning the contents and ends of their ideal academic order. The announcement states "the Talabah (students) of these universities and Madaris (schools) will be entrusted with the duty of *'Jihad-fi-Sabeelillah'* (War in Allah's path) too, and as the heavy responsibility of defending the one and only purely Islamic government in the world will rest on their shoulders, providing aid to these 'Madaris' will be assisting simultaneously in the teaching of Holy Quran and *Hadeeth*, *Jihad-fi-Sabeelillah* (holy war), defense of the Islamic government, implementation of Islamic rule, *Amr-Bil-Ma'roof Wa Nahi-'Anil-Munkar* (enjoin the good, forbid the evil), *Tableegh* and *Da'wah* (propagation and call to Islam) too. Without any doubt, those providing assistance will be blessed with the *'Fadhail'* (merits) of all the above-mentioned departments. Thus this is an excellent and unique opportunity for the Muslims to gather the rewards with both hands." It is reported that Al-Rasheed Trust responded that it had decided to set aside separate funds to be used for education in these Madaris and for their construction only. Books, food and other essentials will also be provided to the Talabah (taliban) of these religious institutions, from these funds, Rasheed Trust confirmed.

It must be argued that implementation of a fully-fledged Islamic system of education is a challenge which the Taliban cannot financially afford at present. As regards to restoring education for girls the Taliban representatives have argued that there are not sufficient funds to provide for girls' education. However, UNICEF stated in a press release on 1, April 1997 that this argument is implausible. The real economic issue is the degree to which the exclusion of girls from schools and women from the workforce is seriously undermining the economic and social development prospects for Afghanistan. Irrespective of financial problems, one can hardly imagine how Taliban could bring in control effects of impartial methodology of modern science which has predominately led to secularism in the Muslim world.

Ethnic and Religious Minorities

The reports produced by witnesses who fled to Pakistan and reports by international human rights investigators indicate on August 8 1998 and the days that followed, the Taliban militiamen and their allies including militant Muslims from neighboring Pakistan systematically executed between 2,000 and 5,000 civilians in one of the deadliest mass killings of civilians in two decades of warfare in Afghanistan. According to some reports the Taliban militiamen searched house to house for males of fighting age who belonged to the Hazara ethnic minority. Hazaras were gunned down in front of their families or had their throats cut. Others, thrown into the city's overcrowded jail, were executed by firing squads or loaded into tractor-trailers, where they sweltered all day in the summer sun, with doors shut, until most perished from suffocation or heat stroke. In the evenings, heavy trucks hauled the bodies to the nearby desert and dumped them in heaps like trash, according to accounts generated by eye witnesses and reported by world media.

Now it is widely believed by independent observers that although the Taliban fought its way to dominance under a unifying banner of

Islam, in ethnic terms its rule represents a return to the pre-communist days of rule by Pashtuns, Afghanistan's largest ethnic group. This belief is amplified by reports to the effect that in taking over Mazar-e-Sharif, the Taliban evidently showed a sectarian twist. The Hazara group is predominantly Shiite Muslim minority; the Taliban is a Sunni Muslim movement. In addition, the Taliban's attack on Mazar-e-Sharif claimed the lives of nine Iranians, provoking Shiite dominated Iran to rattle a big Persian sword on the border, mobilizing tens of thousands of elite troops for military exercises that stretched over an entire month.

Mazar-e-Sharif had remained the last major city holding out against the Taliban's strict rule of Afghanistan, which had included the imposition of Islamic law and tight controls on women. But until the shooting started that Saturday morning in August, few residents had any warning that most of the forces defending Mazar-e-Sharif had slipped away overnight or had defected, leaving the city's gates wide open to the Taliban. As illustrated by reports shock troops arriving in trucks and cars fired automatic weapons at everyone in sight, regardless of ethnicity, in a visible endeavor to frighten a rebellious population into submission.

The Taliban, however, insisted that none of these reports bear the truth about their conquest of Mazar-e-Sharif. The Taliban denounced reports of the international media and humanitarian organizations as "vast propaganda," maintaining that its forces had killed only combatants, confiscated firearms from civilians and temporarily evacuated some residents.

In response to these reports, the Taliban also mentioned the summary executions in May 1997 of an estimated 2,000 to 3,000 Taliban prisoners in the Mazar-e-Sharif area. Notwithstanding this provided the investigators with further reason to believe that those killings motivated the militia to take revenge.

However, Hazaras were not actually responsible for the entire killings. Although they started an uprising soon after the Taliban advanced into the city in an earlier offensive in May 1997, a militia dominated by ethnic Uzbeks quickly took control of the situation and rounded up the Taliban prisoners.

According to some evidence extracted from the Taliban's own words it seems that further to avenging the 1997 killings, the Taliban mass-killing of the Hazaras in August was also because of religious differences and an old blood feud.

Hazaras who survived the onslaught are reported to have been pressured by Niazi, the Taliban commander, to adopt Sunni Muslim rituals, emigrate to Shiite-dominated Iran, pay a special tax as non-Muslims or face death.

Animosity against Shi'ites is admittedly a part of the Taliban's internal propaganda. In the midst of escalation of tension with Iran the following statement publicized by *Dharb-i-Mumin*:

Speaking to a distinguished gathering of eminent `Ulema-e-Kiraam* (respected scholars), *'Alim-e-Deen* (scholar of religion) and *Mufti-e-Azam* (greatest mufti, *fatwa* issuer) of the Taliban Islamic movement Hadhrat Maulana `Abdul 'Ula Deobandi issued a severe warning to Iran saying that if it did not give up its villainy a *'Fatwa'* will be issued against it on the basis of its wicked and corrupt beliefs (shi'ite beliefs), the like of which was issued against Russia. Throwing light upon the Iranian faith, Maulana Deobandi said that dirty-minded and wicked Iranian writers and historians have clearly declared that no one should believe in the Holy Qur'an as, Al-Iyaz-Billah (may God protect us), this book has been compiled by the enemies of *Deen* (religion), the *Sahaba-e-Kiraam* (respected companions of the Prophet) *Radhiallahu Ta`ala `Anhum* (may Allah be pleased with them). They further hold that Hadhrat (his excellency) Ali's name had been mentioned many times in the real Qur'an but the enemies of *Deen* erased it. In reality, Maulana Deobandi said, these beliefs of the Iranians are a direct criticism to a Muslim. Furthermore *'muta'* or *'nikah muwaqqat'*, a Shi'ite tenet, i.e., marriage limited to a certain definite time is, according to the unanimous opinion of religious leaders, clear adultery. Whereas in the Iranian faith it holds the position of a *'sawab'*, or virtuous deed. Maulana Deobandi further said that we have extracts from their authentic books which they cannot deny. He warned Iran that were they to take up the matter of the Iranian beliefs, there would be no *alim* (religious scholar) in the entire Islamic world who would not pass upon them the same *'Fatwa'* passed against Russia during its occupation of Afghanistan. He warned Iran not to test their patience and strength of faith.

With the precedent of inter-religious fights in Islam, one may rightly believe that the natural enemy of a fanatic Sunnite government is a neighboring Shi'ite government. This results in turn in severe arrangements for elimination of local Shi'ites who by being increasingly persecuted may tend to help their fellow Shi'ites in terms of intelligence and prospective military plans.

Civil Rights

The Taliban claim to follow the Islamic code of rights. Duly they hold that the whole conception of human and civil rights must be reinterpreted. What the West understands from these rights are apparently at odds with what Islam prescribes, the Taliban say. The Taliban and fundamentalist Shi'ites in Iran promote the belief that the rights declared as human rights in UN declarations and conventions are not universal. These rights are extracted from the Western thought and therefore are not necessarily in harmony with Islamic views, the Taliban dispute. The main idea is that Islamic performance with regards to imposition of certain lifestyles as well as enforcement of Islamic legal system must not be construed as violation of human and civil rights. The point is when the international organizations accuse the Taliban of ignoring these rights, they are in fact invading the cultural and religious borders of a Muslim nation, the Taliban argue. However it must be discussed that in some cases infringements alleged to have been committed by the Taliban can well be considered as transgressions against universally recognized rights for human beings by Islam.

Some of the violations of which the Taliban are generally accused are as follows:

1. Torture and ill-treatment, including beatings in public places, are widespread.

2. Judicial floggings and amputations were and are carried out.

3. Hundreds of thousands of people were internally displaced or fled the country to become refugees as a result of the Taliban's ethnic policy. It is reported that thousands of civilians, mainly Tajiks, were reportedly forced from their homes by the Taliban, in some

instances by the deliberate destruction of water supply and irrigation systems. Most forcible relocations took place in areas north of Kabul, the capital, including Jabol Seraj, Charikar and Gulbahar, where fierce battles between the Taliban and other forces raged throughout the year.

Likewise thousands of people were reportedly held for periods of up to several months on account of their ethnicity. Among these were around 2,000 Tajik and Hazara men rounded up from their homes in Kabul and held in various jails, including Pul-e-Charkhi Prison in Kabul. Most of them were believed to be prisoners of conscience.

4. Tens of thousands of women remained physically restricted to their homes under the Taliban edicts which continued to ban women from seeking employment, education or leaving home unaccompanied by a male relative. Other measures restricting women included the closure of women's *hammams* (public baths). Women were also barred from the streets for certain periods during the month of Ramadan.

Emma Bonino, the European Commissioner for humanitarian aid, was detained for several hours by the Taliban after members of her entourage visiting Kabul took pictures of women. Hundreds of women were beaten by Taliban guards in detention centers or in public places, including shops, streets and bus stops for defying Taliban edicts.

5. Thousands of men were detained briefly and beaten for alleged un-Islamic behavior or for not complying with policies declared by the Taliban. In July 1997 alone, hundreds of men travelling from Kabul to Kandahar had been punished in accordance with Islamic law for trimming or shaving their beards. Others reported to have been beaten in public included taxi drivers for carrying women passengers, shopkeepers for selling goods to women, children for flying kites or playing other games in the street, and teachers for giving English lessons.

6. Eye-witnesses in Kabul saw men taken from the street and detained in metal transport containers, which are susceptible to extremes of heat and cold. Those who refused to enter were beaten.

7. Sentences of flogging continue to be imposed.

8. Several incidents of amputation were and are still reported.

9. Other sentences of a curious nature are reported including a case in which a woman in the Khair-Khana area of Kabul had the end of her thumb cut off by the Taliban for wearing nail varnish.

10. In September 1997 about 70 civilians, including women and children, were deliberately and arbitrarily killed by armed guards in Qezelabad village near Mazar-e-Sharif. Survivors said the massacre was carried out by Taliban guards retreating from positions they had captured in the area, but Taliban officials denied responsibility for the killing. All the victims reportedly belonged to the Hazara minority. Among the victims was a boy aged about eight who was reportedly killed and decapitated; other victims reportedly had their eyes gouged out with bayonets. Two boys aged about 12 were reportedly held by the guards and had their arms and hands broken with stones.

11. Executions are continuously reported and there has been concern that prisoners of war throughout the country are at risk of execution.

12. Stoning people to death—if found guilty of certain kinds of adultery—continues to be carried out.

As earlier cited an accurate understanding of concepts such as justice, human rights, equality, dignity, honor, brutality and so forth in Islam is of absolute necessity in arguments related to violation of human rights by the Taliban. The truth of the matter is while the Taliban's system of execution of justice is being condemned by many, it has raised a great deal of admiration among other Muslims, governments and individuals.

A hint to what the Taliban considers as human rights is demonstrated in a statement by Sayed Abdur Rahman, a Taliban official and the head of the Shari'a court in Kabul. As regards to substantial number of amputations and similar sentences, he is quoted to have said:

"When we cut the hand of a thief, we have observed human rights...and if infidels criticize us, we say to them that the Quran.. is the guardian of all human beings...If these types of heavenly orders are not enforced, then corruption will increase."

Women and the Taliban Rule

The Taliban announce the imposition of restrictions on women in areas of their domination. These restrictions are considered by the International community in principle to deny Afghan women of their most basic and fundamental human rights, including the right to freedom of association, freedom of expression and employment. Women in Mazar-e-Sharif and elsewhere were ordered through loudspeakers to stay indoors, only to be allowed out in the company of a close male relative and wearing the all-enveloping *burqa*. They were told not to report for work and that education for women and girls was terminated. Such restrictions, since they were first imposed in Taliban controlled areas, have been put in practice by force. One of the persistent policies of the Taliban has been to "punish" women for defying their edicts. In December 1996, Taliban-controlled Radio announced that a group of 225 women had been rounded up and punished in Kabul for violating Taliban rules on clothing. Sources state that punishment of the 225 women consisted of being lashed on the back and legs after the sentence was handed down by a tribunal. Women also continue to be subjected to stoning to death. In March 1997, a woman was reportedly stoned to death in Laghman Province in eastern Afghanistan. According to Radio Voice of Shari'a, the woman who was married had been caught attempting to flee the district with another man. An Islamic tribunal reportedly found her guilty of adultery for which the punishment was death by stoning. Under the Taliban dispensation, women are not allowed to be visible even within the confines of their homes. In March 1997 the Taliban ordered Kabul residents to screen windows in their homes at ground and first floor levels to ensure that women could not be seen from the street. A Taliban representative speaking from the Attorney General's office in Kabul explaining the edict told journalists: "The face of a woman is a source of corruption for men who are not related to them." Women and girls have continued to be barred from attending schools and universities in Taliban controlled areas. On a number of occasions, the Taliban have stated that schooling for women and girls would be restarted when the security situation in the country improved.

However, the Taliban's attitude remains uncompromising. In an interview with *Dharb-i-Mu'min* Maulvi Ehsan-ullah Ehsan, Minister of Finance and Member of Supreme Shura (council) said:

"Enemies of Islam through...'Rights of Women' want to incite women students against Taliban. Thirty-thousand home-confined women are being given salaries by us. Purdah (veil) (is) not the injunction of the Taliban but order of Allah. Objection against it is point-blank *Kufr* (infidelity). In Kabul the Taliban are giving monthly salaries to 30,000 job-free women sitting at home. These are the women who were associated with the anti-Islam mixed system of the Communist and Rabbani era. They had been appointed in offices, colleges and other institutions by the so-called Islamic Government of Rabbani, and were working side by side with men without the Sharee`ah-prescribed *purdah* (veil)". The representative of the Taliban said:

"The Taliban's act of giving monthly salaries to 30,000 job-free women, now sitting comfortably at home, is a whiplash in the face of those who are defaming Taliban with reference to the rights of women. These people through baseless propaganda are trying to incite the women of Kabul against the Taliban."

According to *Dharb*, the Minister claimed that the largest and most developed countries in the world have never helped women in such a way; they have never, only on humanitarian grounds, given salaries to such a vast number of women who are not employed in any office or department but are sitting at home. In answer to another question the member of the Taliban Shura said that the question of women's rights in Kabul has exposed the UNO, Amnesty International and other international organizations for what they are. The minister further commented:

"The world should now know that the UNO and all the other foreign welfare organizations in the name of women's rights are but destroying the society, the culture of the Muslims. Under the veil of 'rights' they want to take away their *purdah*, their veil, and thus dishonor the Muslim women. Their intention is to destroy completely all Islamic values."

In the same interview Maulvi Ehsan-ullah Ehsan warned the women, and specially the female students of Kabul to beware of the evil and dangerous intentions of the 'Christians and Jews'. He said that as a matter of fact the enemies of Islam by planting the seed of hatred in the hearts of brothers and sisters, i.e. the Talibaat (female students) and the Taliban wanted to alienate us from a pious, pure Muslims *Ma`ashirah* (decent association).

The Taliban seem to encounter severe opposition concerning their global recognition in the light of their uncompromising position on gender and other human rights issues in Afghanistan. However it would be quite unlikely for the Taliban leadership to offer concessions even if there is a willingness to do so. This leadership cannot possibly combine its desire to keep its troops prepared to die for Islamic values and at the same time demonstrate liberal flexibility.

7

The Taliban and Afghanistan's Neighbours

Export of the Islamic Caliphate

The concept of exporting the Islamic Caliphate derives from a particular world view that perceives Islamic caliphate as the means whereby Muslims and non-Muslims can liberate themselves from the oppression of tyrants who serve the interests of international imperialism. The United States and its European allies are perceived as the principal imperialist powers that exploit Third World countries. A renewed commitment to Islam, as the experience of the Taliban in overthrowing their opponent powers demonstrated, permits oppressed nations to defeat imperialism. According to this perspective, by following the Taliban example any country can free itself from imperialist domination. Although there exists a general agreement among the Muslim political elite about the desirability of exporting revolutionary Islam, no unanimity exists on the means of achieving this goal. At one end of the spectrum is the view that propaganda efforts to teach Muslims about the Taliban example is the way to export the caliphate. Material assistance of any form is not necessary because oppressed people demonstrate their readiness for an Islamic caliphate by self-motivated revolution against dictatorial governments. Those who subscribe to this line of reasoning argue that the Taliban received no external assistance in setting up their caliphate but were successful as a result of their commitment to Islam. Furthermore, they cite the often stated Taliban dictum that they have no intention of interfering in the internal affairs of other countries. This view is compatible with the maintenance of normal diplomatic relations between Afghanistan and other countries. At the opposite end of the spectrum is the view of the Taliban as the only true patron of a world revolutionary movement to liberate Muslim countries specifically, and other Third World countries generally, from imperialist subjugation. This activist perspective contends that the effective export of the caliphate must not be limited to propaganda efforts but must also include both financial and military assistance to so-called liberation movements. Advocates of this view also cite Quranic verses and prophetic sayings to justify their position and frequently quote scriptural statements on the inevitability of the spread of the Islamic caliphate throughout the world.

In a statement issued by Mufti Rasheed Ahmad Sahib from Darul Ifta-e-Wal Irshad, Karachi, it is stated:

"It is compulsory and a debt upon Muslims to provide moral, political, military and financial support to the heroes of Islam, "The Taliban" who are free from the destructive yoke of the World Bank, IMF, UN and others. Remember! Only "The Taliban" can help the Islamic World out of their internal and external crisis."

Anti-Islam forces are bending over backwards to economically crush this new born pure Islamic state before it becomes a world economic power.

Will the conscience of Muslims, their Islamic honour, and their religious ardour continue to tolerate this situation? "The Taliban" has exalted the Muslim *Ummah* with the establishment of pure Islam. The Taliban has also helped the families of the *Shaheed* (killed fighting for God), war orphans, the dispossessed, the displaced and the needy people of Kabul.

The Taliban of Afghanistan

1. Who have after centuries established the only Government of Islam on the lines of Khilafat-e-Rashidah (righteous caliphate).
2. Who, spurning world pressure on all fronts, internally, externally, militarily and economically, implemented the Laws of Islam over the area they govern.
3. Whose Government is not being recognised because of committing the crime of implementing Islam in its purest form.

4. Who expelled India and its ally, Russia from Kabul.
5. Whose Governors, Commanders and Ministers are working without salaries just for the sake of Allah Ta'ala (i.e. *Fi-Sabi-Lillah*).
6. Who saved the fruits of a magnificent fourteen-year old jihad from going to waste.
7. Whose jihad in the Path of Allah is more superior and holier than any other jihad going on in the world today.
8. Whose aid in military, economic, moral and every other kind of help is a *fardh* (religious obligation) upon all the Muslims of the world.
9. Who in helping you will not only help the Mujahideen (Muslim fighters) but also orphans, widows, immigrants (Muhajireen), the poor and the needy.
10. Who require the help not of the *Kuffar* (the heathen) but that of the Muslims, for it is the need of the Muslims themselves.
11. Who best deserve *Zakah, 'Ushr, Sadaqat-e-Wajibah* and *Nafilah* (various types of Islamic levies and charitable payments)."

In this context, a religious inquiry directed to Fazal Mohammad Sahib about the identity of the Taliban seems to be interesting and guiding. He was asked "Who are the Taliban? How did this group emerge? How did they Advance?" He replied:

"Taliban is the mercy which Allah Ta'ala (the transcendent) has sent to the people of Afghanistan in exchange for their sacrifices. Insha-Allah they will become the source of honour and dignity for all the oppressed Muslims of the world and a mercy for the religion of Islam."

It appears that a good number of these questions are not merely seeking to identify the nature and function of the Taliban but are aimed rather at advertising them through the legitimacy and authenticity contained in the answers. To these *ulema*, the Taliban mission is a global one. Afghanistan is only the first stage. However, they admit that unlike Iran, the Taliban are deprived of sources of wealth and they have to take their time until they are financially capable of launching massive efforts in spreading their message. The statements frequently released by official Taliban sources are also indicative of an inclination towards world domination within the Movement. It is of paramount importance to discover the manners through which they seek to dominate and consolidate their authority in other regions. In a communication made on behalf of the Taliban Department of Education to Rasheed Trust, it is stated:

"From Kabul, capital of the Islamic Emirate, minister of information and member of Supreme *Shura* Mulla Ameer Khan Muttaqi has informed Al-Rasheed Trust on behalf of the Ministry of Education that in accordance with the directives of *Ameeral-M'umineen* (Commander of the Faithful), new universities and colleges are being opened to provide higher education to ten thousand students in each province of Qandhar, Kabul, Herat and Jalalabad, and new Madaris (plural form of madrasa, seminary) are being established for five hundred students in each of the other eighteen provinces. Al-Rasheed Trust should now come forward to assist in the completion of this noble, purely religious work.

As the Talabah of these universities and Madaris will be entrusted with the duty of '*Jihad-fi-Sabeelillah*' (holy war in Allah's path) too, and as the heavy responsibility of defending the one and only purely Islamic government in the world will rest on their shoulders, providing aid to these 'Madaris' will be assisting simultaneously in the teaching of Holy Quran and *Hadeeth, Jihad-fi-Sabeelillah*, defence of the Islamic government, implementation of Islamic rule, *Amr-Bil-Ma`roof Wa Nahi- Anil-Munkar, Tableegh* and *Da`wah* too. Without any doubt, those providing assistance will be blessed with the '*Fadhail*' of all the above-mentioned departments. Thus, this is an excellent and unique opportunity for Muslims to gather the rewards with both hands.

The Management of Al-Rasheed Trust has decided to set aside separate funds to be used for education in these Madaris and for their construction only. Books, food and other essentials will also be provided to the Talabah of these religious institutions, from these funds."

The Taliban have already indicated what they mean when they are speaking of jihad. They attacked a government in Kabul which was built on many years of Islamic jihad. This government, led by Rabbani, presented itself as an Islamic government and had been recognised worldwide as such. It is a known fact that, theologically, the Taliban needed to discredit the Islamic government of Rabbani in order to furnish their claims for political domination with legitimate grounds. Afghanistan's neighbours, including Iran, take that point into account and base their relationship with the Taliban on it. By claiming to be the only pure Islamic government in the world the Taliban would certainly be in a position to attract massive numbers of Islamic members of opposition groups all over the Islamic world. There are three characteristics which place the Taliban in a distinguished stronghold and grant them a superior ability to successfully conduct a full fledged campaign against what they call corrupt Islamic regimes.

1. In contrast to the neighbouring Islamic government of Iran, they are not representing a minority within the larger community of the faithful. They are Sunnites and possess a more powerful theological medium to get their message across.

2. Contrary to the Saudi example of an Islamic government that was confronted with dismay from its early periods due to its political system which is based on the Wahhabi school and monarchy, the Taliban are from the extensively popular Hanafite schools and their political system is advertised to be founded on purely Islamic conceptions of caliphate.

3. In cultural terms, the Taliban exemplify a wider range of ethnic and denominational groups. Ethnically, they epitomise the powerful Pashtun people who are widespread in Afghanistan, Pakistan and India. Within the same context, they are closely associated with other ethnic groups existing in the region and occupying extensive parts of eastern Iran and western India. Many of the Taliban leaders and theologians are graduates of schools with Saudi educational systems and many of them are highly qualified in Arabic culture and history. They therefore typify a dynamic bond with the Arab world.

The Taliban and Pakistan

Since the Taliban took control of Kabul in September 1996 they have been calling for international recognition of their administration. Following the Taliban's capture of Mazar-e-Sharif, Pakistan became the first country to officially recognise the Taliban administration as the government of Afghanistan. Pakistan is known to support the Taliban and many observers believe that this includes military assistance, despite Pakistan's denial of such assertions. Saudi Arabia and the United Arab Emirates also formally recognised the Taliban administration as the government in Afghanistan.

There are reports which verify the presence of Pakistani troops within the Taliban militia. For instance, refugees from Mazar-e-Sharif reported that the Taliban were accompanied by Pakistani fighters identifiable by their language, dress and the flag of a Pakistani Muslim fundamentalist party aligned with the Taliban.

In August 1998, the Russian Government accused Pakistan of taking part in a Taliban offensive in the north of Afghanistan. In a direct statement, which seemed to be well investigated, Russia said that Pakistan's military was directly involved in fighting and in supplying the Taliban with equipment.

A Russian spokesman, Valery Nesterushkin, said that the opposition alliance in the north had captured numerous Pakistani servicemen on the battlefields. The Iranian government had indicated a reluctance to Pakistani contribution to the Taliban fighting machine ever since they came to occupy extensive lands. Similar reports about the presence of Pakistani troops in the Taliban army were and are repeatedly reported by Iranian sources.

In November 1998, the Prime Minister Nawaz Sharif of Pakistan was reported as calling for the introduction of Taliban style rapid Islamic justice in Pakistan, including hanging rapists within 24 hours, in a move that stunned opposition and human rights groups. According to reports, Sharif said: "Today in Afghanistan, crimes have virtually come to naught. I have heard that one can safely drive a vehicle full of gold at midnight without fear", "I want this kind of system in Pakistan. Justice will end oppression and bring prosperity", "Murderers and rapists roam around freely for years. Such people should be hanged publicly and their cases decided in 24 hours, three days or seven days."

Sharif's words were often interpreted in the light of his domestic problems with the Pakistani Senate as well as the opposition.

However, various interpretations based on the internal political situation in Pakistan cannot ignore the literal implications of these words. What is clear is that the Pakistani premier was very pleased with the Taliban ways of executing justice. He admired them for their achievements which were made possible only through executions, floggings and amputations. Sharif's comments spontaneously supplied the aforesaid reports and statements made by various governments and organisations with logical foundations. According to these comments, recognition of the Taliban administration by Pakistan is not merely because the Taliban virtually control all of Afghanistan, but also because they represent a system which is both approved and admired by the Pakistani administration.

However, one must note that the outlook of the former Pakistani premier is echoing the desire of many religious and political groups in Pakistan. These people represent a huge political power of which Nawaz Sharif was fully aware. These are the very same groups whose pressures push Pakistani governments into wars of words and at times wars of armies with India over the Kashmir issue. Nevertheless, one must bear in mind that this issue is sometimes used in reverse to stimulate internal modes of anger or excitement by Pakistani governments. As regards Afghan problems there is a semi consensus amongst these groups that during the cold war Russia and India were brought closer to each other by material and ideological links. India, which has always posed a danger to Pakistan, became a constant headache for this country as the main strategic American ally. Russians needed to draw over to their side Afghanistan, in order to gain direct advantages as well as to create problems for Pakistan. These groups believe that the Russians, by invading Afghanistan, achieved their goal and that their next target would be Pakistan. This is a belief which was shared by a large number of Pakistanis and amplified by Western sources.

It is understood from sources close to the Taliban that the first 'Fatwa' concerning the jihad of Afghanistan was given in Pakistan by Sheikh-ul-Hadeeth, Maulana `Abdul Haq and Maulana Mufti Mahmood sahib.

The interest in Afghanistan is not merely a matter of political and circumstantial events. Pakistani interest is deeply rooted in the ethnic, cultural and religious structures shared by the two countries.

Almost all the people of Pakistan are Muslims. Most of them belong to the Sunnite sect, the major branch of Islam, with a significant representation among the Shiite branch. The majority of Pakistani Sunnites, like most of the Afghans, belong to the orthodox Hanafite school, which is one of four schools or subsects of Sunnism. In Pakistan, those who are trained in theology are given the title of mullah or *mawlana* or, collectively, *ulema*. Similar to Afghanistan, there are powerful hereditary networks of "holy men" called *pirs* who receive great reverence as well as gifts in cash or kind from a multitude of followers. An established *pir* may pass on his spiritual powers and sanctified authority to one or more of his *murids* ("disciples"), who may then operate as a *pir* in his own right.

Ethnically, Pashtuns constitute the majority of the population of Afghanistan. They are Pashto-speaking people of south eastern Afghanistan and north western Pakistan. Several Pashtun tribes are known to have moved from Afghanistan to Pakistan between the 13th and 16th century. Each tribe, consisting of kinsmen who trace descent in the male bloodline from a common tribal ancestor, is divided into clans, subclans, and patriarchal families. Tribal genealogies establish rights of succession and inheritance as well as the right to use tribal lands and to speak in tribal council. Disputes over property, women, and personal injury often result in blood feuds between families and whole clans; which may be inherited unless settled by the intervention of clan chiefs or by tribal council. Pashtuns are farmers, herdsmen, and warriors. Most tribesmen are sedentary farmers, combining cultivation with animal husbandry, some are migratory herdsmen and caravaners. Large numbers of them have always been attracted to military service. There are estimated to be about 8,000,000 Pashtun in Afghanistan and 2,000,000 in Pakistan. In Afghanistan, where the Pashtun are the predominant ethnic group, the main tribes—or, more accurately, federations of tribes—are the Durrani south of Kabul and the Ghilzay east of Kabul. In Pakistan, the Pashtun predominate north of Quetta between the Sulaiman Range and the Indus River.

In Afghanistan and Pakistan where tribal law is still final in tribal life the political borders have born very little meaning to the people of the same tribes living on opposite sides of these borders. However, this has caused tensions between Afghanistan and Pakistan at times. A glimpse of the conflict over Pashtun inhabited areas is certainly helpful in drawing a comprehensive picture of the events which have led to contemporary policy on Pakistan in Afghanistan.

In 1947 the Afghan government closely scrutinised the events that attended the establishment of India and Pakistan as independent states. Of particular concern, then, of the Afghan government was the incorporation into Pakistan of the North-West Frontier Province Tribal Areas, a neighbouring region largely populated by Pashtun. Pakistan ignored Afghan demands for a plebiscite in the Tribal Areas on the question of self-determination. Retaliating, in 1947 Afghanistan voted against the admission of Pakistan to the United Nations. Relations between the two countries continued to be strained during the next several years. Sporadic frontier clashes occurred between Pakistani forces and Pashtun tribesmen, especially after 1949, when the latter, with the approval of the Afghan government, launched a movement to establish an independent state to be called Pashtunistan or Pathanistan.

Afghanistan manifested displeasure over a US-Pakistan military aid pact concluded in 1954. The following year Soviet Premier Nikolai A. Bulganin, visiting Afghanistan, proclaimed support for a state of Pashtunistan. Subsequently the USSR and Afghanistan issued a joint statement advocating peaceful coexistence, universal disarmament, and United Nations membership for China. The Soviet government simultaneously extended technical-aid loans to Afghanistan.

The Taliban provides Pakistan with a number of solutions. By stabilising Afghanistan they make it possible for Pakistan to give assurances to both Central Asian Republics and Western investors that Karachi is the obvious choice to be the port of trade starting from Central Asia and passing through Afghanistan. The Taliban may also help keep the hell raising activities of rebellious tribesmen at the borders under control. Another contribution of the Taliban might manifest itself in relieving Pakistan of the burden of Afghan refugees. And last but not least in the list of possible contributions of the Taliban to Pakistan's regional and international policies is to help keep Iran, and most importantly India, busy in future. However, the Taliban might turn into a double-edged sword with the sharper edge directed to Pakistan itself.

1. With the Pashtun dominance and majority in Afghanistan, a Pashtun government may be seen as a natural resort by a minority suffering from insecurity and inequality in Pakistan.

2. From an Islamic point of view, the interaction on two sides of the borders is ongoing on an equal basis. With the institutionalisation of a religiously devoted Hanafite government in Afghanistan coupled with a well-funded system of religious education, the immigration and emergence of eminent scholars and talented students to and in Afghanistan would be a logical result. Independence in religious matters, together with a strong sense of tribal and patriotic attachments will amplify the desire in Afghans to assert their existence as an independent entity and the only source of Islamic enlightenment to the world. This religious tycoon cannot pin great hopes on either Shi'ite Iran nor Russian backed Central Asians. The only available arena for Taliban manoeuvres would be Pakistan, where they already have all the ingredients of success, including the convenience of language, Pashtun human forces, Hanafite Islam, fundamentalist sympathisers, and well-established financial and educational institutions already at hand, as well as, importantly, relatively widespread political chaos.

Finally, the following is an advertisement consistent with the issue of Taliban links with Pakistan.

Deputy Foreign Minister of the Islamic Emirate of Afghanistan, Mulla `Abdul Jaleel has asked Al-Rasheed Trust to make arrangements, like the previous year, for the *Qurbani* (sacrifices) of animals on the occasion of `Eid-ul-Adhha to be offered in Kabul, thus helping the needy, the Muhajireen, Mujahideen and families of the *Shuhada*. According to the deputy minister a vast number of destitute Muhajireen of the northern areas, residing in Kabul, Herat, Helmand, and Kandhar are in desperate need of every kind of help and assistance.

Al-Rasheed Trust requests all Muslims in general, supporters of the Taliban, and readers of *Dha'rb-i-M'umin* in particular, to offer their '*Wajib*' and '*Nafl*' *Qurbani*, in Kabul, Herat, Badghis and Kandhar on the occasion of 'Eid-ul-Adhha. Besides the '*Wajib*' (compulsory) of Qurbani, they would thus be discharging their '*Fardh*' of helping the poor and needy, the Taliban Mujahideen, families of the *Shuhada*, as well as thousands of destitute widows and orphans.

According to Mulla 'Abdul Jalil Sahib, the cost of a medium sheep is Pak. Rs. 3,000/ or U.K. Pounds 40/ or U.S. Dollars 65/, only.

The cost of the *Qurbani* can be deposited in the Trust's branches in Lahore, Rawalpindi, Peshawar, Mansehra, Mingora and its central office in Karachi.

Contacts:

1. Karachi: Al-Rasheed Trust, Kitab Ghar, Opposite *Darul Ifta-e-Wal Irshad*, Nazimabad 4, Karachi. Post Code: 74600. Phone: 6683301. Fax: 021-623666. Account no: 42457-74. Dollar Account no: 55017-41. Pound Account no: 065001-38. Habib Bank Limited, Foreign Exchange Branch, Habib Square, Karachi.

2. Rawalpindi: Office *Dha'rb-i-M'umin*, Room no. 3, Third Floor, Moti Plaza, Near Liaquat Bagh, Murree Road, Rawalpindi. Temporary Phone no: 05772-2827. Temporary Fax no: 051-554788. From 6: 00 p.m to 11: 00 p.m.

3. Lahore: Mufti Ghulam Mustafa Sahib, Jamia Masjid, Sulaiman Park, Begum Pura, Lahore. Phone no: 042-6812081.

4. Mingora: Maulvi 'Abdul Baseer, Office *Dha'rb-i-M'umin*, Top Floor, Dr Dawa Khan Dental Clinic Surgeon, Main Bazar, Mingora, Swat. Temporary Phone no: 0936-6147.

5. Mansehra: Maulvi 'Obaid-ur-Rahman, Maulvi Muhammad Sadiq, Office *Dha'rb-i-M'umin*, Opposite Khyber Bank, Abbottabad Road, Mansehra. Temporary Phone no: 0987-36513, 37491.

6. Peshawar: Maulvi Akhtar 'Ali, Office *Dha'rb-i-M'umin*, Z. R. Brothers, Katchehry Road, Chowk Yadgaar, Peshawar. Temporary Phone no: 091-210249.

The Taliban and Iran

Iran and Pakistan are two important neighbours of Afghanistan which have contributed hugely in shaping the political and cultural statistics of this country. Having said that, Afghanistan, if considered as an independent entity throughout history, has had its own considerable impact on the region in general and its western and southern neighbouring lands in particular. A pursuit of the cultural interaction between Afghanistan and Iran clearly indicates that in some aspects, including the cultural and literal and to some extent the civilisational dimensions, the history of Iran cannot be looked at independently from that of Afghanistan. An example of this fact manifests itself in the significance of Rumi as the most eminent Sufi poet of Persian literature. Rumi, who is known to the West, is undoubtedly the main pillar of the mystical literature of the Iranians.

Jalal ad-din Rumi (1207-73) is the greatest of the Islamic mystic poets in the Persian language whose disciples founded an order of mystics known as Whirling Dervishes. The basis of Islamic mysticism, called Sufism in Western languages, is the attempt, by meditation, to comprehend the nature of God and man and to experience the divine presence in the world. The most excellent and detailed poetic expression of this made Jalal ad-din the most outstanding of the Sufi writers in Persian history and the literal hero and cultural icon of Iranians for centuries.

However, Jalal ad-Din was born in what is now Afghanistan on about September 30, 1207. His father was a theologian and teacher. The family left their home in about 1218 and traveled to Anatolia in Asia Minor to escape the threat of the Mongol invasion from the East. In 1228 they settled at Konya, the capital. His father taught at a religious school until his death in 1231, when Jalal took over the teaching. Jalal remained in Konya as a poet and teacher until his death on December 17, 1273.

Rumi epitomises just one example of the perpetual flux of interaction between Iran and Afghanistan. Cities such as Balkh, Qandahar and Herat are still popularly considered as Iranian territories. This has not been a product of an Iranian political agenda. Rather, this is an impression which infiltrates Iranian minds and hearts when they go through their literal heritage, whose best manifestations are *divans* of eminent Persian poets such as Hafiz and Sa'di of Shiraz. The glories of these areas are excellently depicted by these poets and one does not feel that these poets are talking about foreign lands and that these lands are at all different from other Iranian areas. The truth of the matter is that even in an era when these poets illustrated these towns in their works there existed no central government unifying all these geographical locations. However, the fact that the movement of people was not confined within what is currently known as political borders, as well as the instability of constantly changing governments, made Persian culture and literature the only genuine factor of affiliation and solidarity between people separated from each other geographically.

The identical parts of history of Iran and Afghanistan are not merely restricted to cultural aspects. There are further political events which are popularly shared by them. The chronicle of the dynasties that ruled Iran constitutes a principal part of the schools' academic curriculum adopted by the Iranian government, the account of the Ghaznavid dynasty has always been studied and regarded as one of the above mentioned dynasties. The contribution of this dynasty both to Iranian culture and history is recorded in books dealing with Iranian history. Even the conquest of India by Mahmud, the better known king of this dynasty, is regarded by some Iranians as a matter of national pride. Popular legends have been woven around his heroic personality and stories of his courageous conquests have moved down through generations to contemporary Iran.

The factual data is that in the middle of the 10th century a former Turkish slave named Alptegin seized Ghazna and was succeeded by another former slave, Subuktigin, who extended the conquests to Kabul and the Indus. His son was the great Mahmud of Ghazna, who came to the throne in 998. Mahmud conquered the Punjab and Multan and carried his raids into the heart of India. The hitherto obscure town of Ghazna became a splendid city, as did the second capital at Bust.

The reason why Mahmud is not called or even regarded as an "Afghan" king by Iranians may be rooted in the cultural grounds which were referred to earlier. For them there has been historically one Iran which happened to be ruled by rulers from various ethnic origins. This is an image from Mahmud which was shared by Ferdowsi, whom the Iranians regard as the greatest of their poets. For nearly a thousand years they have continued to read and to listen to recitations from Ferdowsi's master work, the *Shah-nameh*, in which the Persian national epic found its final and enduring form. Though written about 1,000 years ago, this work is as intelligible to the average, modern Iranian as the King James version of the Bible is to a modern English-speaker. The language, based as poem on a Pahlavi original, is pure Persian with only the slightest admixture of Arabic. European scholars have criticised this enormous poem for what they have regarded as its monotonous metre, its constant repetitions, and its stereotyped similes; but to the Iranian it is the history of his country's glorious past, preserved for all time in sonorous and majestic verse.

The *Shah-nameh*, finally completed in 1010, was presented to the celebrated Sultan Mahmud of Ghazna who by that time had made himself master of Ferdowsi's homeland, Khurasan. Information on the relations between poet and patron is largely legendary. According to Nezami-ye Aruzi, Ferdowsi came to Ghazna in person and through the good offices of the minister Ahmad ibn Easan Meymandi was able to secure the Sultan's acceptance of the poem. Unfortunately, Mahmud then consulted certain enemies of the minister as to the poet's reward. They suggested that Ferdowsi should be given 50,000 dirhams, and that even this was too much, in view of his heretical Shi'ite tenets. Mahmud, a bigoted Sunnite, was influenced by their words, and in the end Ferdowsi received only 20,000 dirhams. Bitterly disappointed, he went to a public bath and, on coming out, divided the whole of the money between the bath attendants!

Perhaps traces of conflict between Persian speakers living in two adjacent areas start manifesting themselves in this piece of history. The Sunnism of the king leads to a row between him and the great poet. This issue has remained as a hindrance, separating people with common language. This is subsequently the reason beyond the Iranians' failure to strengthen their position in Afghanistan throughout the recent period. As regards the recent tension between the Taliban and Iran in the aftermath of the killing of Iranian diplomats, it would be immediately noticed that religious emotions sprung up to deepen the aspects of hostilities.

In a religious inquiry (*istifta*) published in *Dharb*, a newspaper close to the Taliban, Mulla Mohammad Umar, the leader of the Taliban, asks a number of scholars questions of significance concerning the Taliban's rule in Afghanistan as well their relationship with Iran. He asked:

"If Iran or any other country carries out military aggression against our land, will our defensive action be termed as 'ordinary war' or 'jihad' (holy war)?"

The scholars answered:

"We are of the opinion that if our neighbour Iran attacks our soil, especially when it has no reason or justification for doing so, defending our country against it will be called *Shara`ee* (religiously legitimate) jihad and not ordinary war."

Umar again asks:

"Will the defence of the country be a *Fardh* (religious obligation) upon the armed forces only or upon all those who have no Shara`ee excuse, and are able to defend the land?

The answer is:

"In case of an attack jihad will be a *Fardh-i-`Ain* (collective religious obligation), upon every Muslim citizen of the Emirate. It will be incumbent upon every Muslim to go forth for jihad.

Umar questions:

"In case of an attack, when the enemy forces are defeated is it enough to push them out of the borders of the country, or is it permissible to chase them within their own borders too?"

The response is:

"If the enemy is not completely vanquished, and its armed forces are still fighting, Afghanistan can order pursuing the enemy inside its own territory as well as military action within its boundaries."

Umar adds:

"For the defence of its territory and Islamic system, can the Islamic Emirate seek the help of other Islamic and non-Islamic countries?"

The *ulema* further comment:

"Whether the Islamic Emirate seeks the help of other Muslim countries or not, it is incumbent upon them to help it in defending its borders. In case of need, unconditional help can be solicited from non-Muslim countries too."

Up to this point, the scholars are not making a distinction between the Iranians and the Sunnite Mujahideen in Afghanistan in terms of letting the Taliban treat them in the harshest manner. This is evidently due to their belief that the Taliban are representing Islam exclusively and that they are liable to take action against anything or anybody in order to achieve their purposes. However, the philosophy behind these answers goes farther to include the typical Sunnite arguments against Shi'ism. This is evident from the words of Abdul 'Ula Deobandi who is quoted immediately after the above answers and questions as saying:

Speaking to a distinguished gathering of eminent `Ulema-e-Kiraam (respected clergymen), 'Alim-e-Deen (scholar of religion) and Mufti-e-Azam (the greatest source of religious answers) of the Taliban Islamic movement Hadhrat Maulana Abdul 'Ula Deobandi issued a severe warning to Iran saying that if it did not give up its villainy, a 'Fatwa' will be issued against it on the basis of its wicked and corrupt beliefs, the like of which was issued against Russia. Throwing light upon the Iranian faith, Maulana Deobandi said that dirty-minded and wicked Iranian writers and historians have clearly declared that no one should believe in the Holy Qur'an as this book has been compiled by the enemies of Deen (Islamic faith), the Sahaba-e-Kiraam (respected companions of the Prophet) Radhiallahu Ta`ala `Anhum (may God be pleased with them). They further hold that Imam Ali's name had been mentioned many times in the real Qur'an but the enemies of Deen erased it. In reality, Maulana Deobandi said, these beliefs of the Iranians are a direct criticism of Islam itself. Furthermore 'muta' or 'nikah muwaqqat', i.e. marriage limited to a certain definite time is, according to the unanimous opinion of the religious leaders, clear adultery, whereas in the Iranian faith it holds the position of a 'sawab', or virtuous deed. Maulana Deobandi further said that we have extracts from their authentic books which they cannot deny. He warned Iran that were they to take up the matter of the Iranian beliefs, there would be no alim (clergyman) in the entire Islamic world who would not pass upon them the same

'*Fatwa*' passed against Russia during its occupation of Afghanistan. He warned Iran too not to test their patience and strength of faith. Iran was not as powerful as Moscow. He further reminded Iran that Allah Ta`ala had destroyed Pharaoh and Haman. Could He not destroy Iran too? If the enemy is strong, Allah is even stronger. He asked Iran not to be proud of its military power. The unarmed Afghans had defeated an enemy as mighty as the Soviet Union. With the help of Allah they would vanquish Iran too Insha Allah, if they dared to attack them.

However, the Iranian outlook seems to be based more on political grounds. They have publicly proclaimed that their opposition to the Taliban is due to their belief that the Taliban misrepresents Islam, they have violated human rights as well as the international law. Iranians also further commented that the Taliban, by physically eliminating their political opponents, proved to be undemocratic. The only religious issue which appears to be of relevance to Iranians is that to them the Taliban are misrepresenting Islam and by doing so they bring disrepute on Islam world wide. Despite the fact that Iranians have not formally specified the kind of Islam which to them is misrepresented by the Taliban, it would be out of context if one assumes that they mean by this the Shi'ite Islam. Circumstantial evidence shows that Iranians have the Hanafite Islam as represented by Mujahideen in mind. This Iranian stance is certainly the result of twenty years of international diplomatic experience. Through their past repeated failures they have learned to build their international cases on issues which address the universal common sense, issues such as human rights, democracy and recently, the "dialogue between civilisations". Nevertheless, the Iranians soon realised that this is not an arena for political manoeuvres and that the Taliban needed to be shown some more convincing arguments. Mobilisation of Iranian troops on borders was apparently the winning card and theTaliban soon figured out that military logic may not have been operative and that they needed to review their political performance. The truth of the matter is that the Taliban, as they have repeatedly said, strive to bring an end to their internal and international problems via conquering the entire country. They are well acquainted with the fact that as soon as they achieve total domination they would be recognised as the legitimate government of Afghanistan. As it has been observed elsewhere, international recognition turned them overnight from criminal outlaws to respected statesmen. Therefore instead of time and energy consuming political disputes through which they are certainly expected to offer concessions, they have preferred to consolidate their power and as a result delete the necessity of talks. Notwithstanding this Iranians and other dissatisfied players in Afghanistan were and still are fully aware of the implications of the Taliban's complete supremacy. As regards Iran, the Taliban are mindful of a number of facts.

1. The Taliban's most effective weapon, namely jihad, may not satisfy the requirements of a fully fledged war with Iran. That is due to the fact that Iran is likewise being led by Muslim clergymen who are capable of providing their troops with religious motivations. The Taliban realises that in such a conflict with equally religiously motivated troops they would be highly likely to loose.

2. The Persian culture has always been in a superior position in Afghanistan. Speaking Persian is both a necessity and a sign of a high culture. A large number of Pashtun people speak fluent Persian and have been exposed to Persian culture. Likewise one has to bear in mind that the Persian centre of cultural and literal productivity in that region is Iran and in a modern course of cultural inter-penetration the upper hand would be Iran's. Hundreds of thousands of Afghans now have a new loyalty and allegiance to Iran. These are Afghan children who were born in Iran in exile and have never known any other country. With both Islamic identity, which is likely to be more moderate in ensuing years, and Persian culture supplemented with oil generated wealth and military supremacy, the Taliban leaders are aware of the consequences of a long conflict and edgy relationship with Iran.

3. As a token of good will, former Pakistani foreign minister informed his Iranian counterpart that Pakistan was not pleased to have its ties with Iran negatively affected by the Taliban issue. He further remarked that more and more control over Afghanistan affairs was being transferred from the military establishment to the prime minister and political leadership of Pakistan. Regardless of

what happened to this balance after the *coup* in Pakistan, the fact is that with Iranian President Khatami's arms opened to embrace Arab neighbours as well as open its market to European and (very likely) American companies on a massive scale, the Taliban must acknowledge that taking advantage of Iran's global isolation might no longer be a reliable possibility. In this new balance of powers they must admit that in a world prevailed by economic and political considerations today's priority may not be that of tomorrow and current allies may turn their back on them to seek the favour of the wealthier and more lubricant market, Iran.

These points are not merely theoretical conclusions reached through speculative study of this case. These are realities which the Taliban have to face. Perhaps their comprehension of these points led them to demonstrate flexibility in their talks with the UN envoy concerning the crisis with Iran. The Taliban know at this stage that their political future depends either on immediate international recognition or completely subduing their adversaries. These are inter-related by the fact that surviving resistance supported by Iran hinders them in achieving complete domination and at the same time resistance forces representing the recognised government of the Mujahideen provide them with no grounds internally to claim legitimacy.

India and China

In a statement issued by Mufti Rasheed Ahmad Sahib, Darul Ifta-e-Wal Irshad, Karachi, there exists a set of goals which are to be achieved by the Taliban.

'A Momentaring Error, Punish for Centuries'
By: Mufti 'Azam Hazrat Maulana Mufti Rasheed Ahmad Sahib, Darul Ifta-e-Wal Irshad
"It is compulsory and a debt upon Muslims to provide moral, political, military and financial support to the heroes of Islam", 'The Taliban' who are free from the destructive yoke of the World Bank, IMF, UN and others.

Remember! Only The Taliban can help the Islamic World out of their internal and external crisis.

Anti-Islam forces are bending over backwards to economically crush this new born pure Islamic state, before it becomes a world economic power...

The Taliban of Afghanistan are those who expelled India and its ally, Russia from Kabul."

The cynical insight of Pakistanis on both popular and formal levels to India is not a new phenomena. To many Pakistani *ulema*, *Hunud* (Hindus) are as vicious as the Jews. It is observed in some of their prayers. The *ulema* would say "O Lord, damn the Hindus and the Jews". However, it may be argued that despite the weight of the mentioned resentment, there might be further reasons for associating Indians with Russia in the latter's invasion of Afghanistan. This outlook may have its roots in the geopolitics of the region during the cold war. In the face of perpetual Pakistani challenges backed by the United States, an anti-colonialist India would find alliance with the Soviet Union as a normal choice. Therefore, in years of tension over Kashmir and killings in the Muslim population in India, the Russians would be held as partners in crime by Pakistan. There is little doubt about the united front of the United States and Pakistan in their confrontational invasion of the Soviet Union in Afghanistan. This means that India has to take extra care concerning an increasing American need for Pakistan to keep Russians from progressing southward. On the other hand, Russia has shown an awareness of the weak point between the two neighbouring countries by offering Indians more tempting commercial packages. Afghanistan is no longer a Russian stronghold. Rather it is now a reliable ally of Pakistan. This is most certainly a source of political perturbation and unease to India. India cannot possibly afford to undergo further sectarian violence within it's territories. Indians are fully aware of the consequence of bloody encounters sponsored and religiously justified by another neighbour state.

In contrast to the Indian situation, China, in accordance with their known political orientation, was not at all pleased with Russian subjugation of the whole of central Asia and beyond. As a matter of fact, Chinese rule in deciding the future of Afghanistan during the years of Soviet invasion was decisive and drastic. During the conflict with the Soviets the only weapons systems that solidly continued to bedevil the resistance were combat helicopter gunships and jet bombers. Toward the end of 1986, however, the resistance fighters began to receive more and better weapons from the outside world, particularly from the United States, the United Kingdom, and China via Pakistan, the most important of these being shoulder fired ground-to-air missiles. The Soviet and Afghan air forces then began to suffer considerable casualties. The impact of the supplies provided by powers like China was definitely fatal. As always, China is by no means indifferent to the Afghan polemic. With the Muslim population excessive in number to those of some Islamic main lands, and also with an eye to the spread of American influence in neighbouring Afghanistan, China cannot connive with indifference in the current struggle.

At the time of writing, based on the latest reports a Chinese military delegate is visiting Afghanistan to investigate the methods of military co-operation with the Taliban.

Central Asian Neighbours of Afghanistan

Afghanistan is no longer a country bordering Russia. Since the collapse of the former Soviet Union, new countries have emerged to constitute the new neighbours of Afghanistan. These countries are not homogenous religiously and ethnically with one another or with Afghanistan. It might be too early to talk in detail about the foreign policies of these countries toward the Taliban. This is due to the fact that most of them are still experiencing periods of social instability and political unrest. Whatever the case with these countries may be, there is one point upon which there exists a general agreement. That is to say that the present ruling parties are not in favour of stirring up their internal vicissitudes by openly taking sides in the Afghanistan dilemma. In Tajikistan, the Tajik people make up more than half of the population. They speak a form of Persian called Tajik and are Muslims, as are their close neighbors, the Uzbeks. There are other ethnic groups in the population including Uzbeks, Russians, Tatars, Germans, and Ukrainians. However, Persian culture prevails and the country's ties with Iran have been over emphasized since gaining independence from the Soviet Union. Iranians have invested extensively in Tajikistan's cultural, social and economic life. Tajiks form a major minority in Afghanistan and Rabbani, the president of the Islamic State of Afghanistan, is a Tajik. The main force of resistance against the Taliban is also led by a Tajik, Ahmad Shah Masoud. Therefore, these parameters, together with the Taliban's treatment of Afghan Tajiks, would certainly be taken into account in their relationship with Tajikistan. Tajikistan, under the leadership of Rahmanove, has indicated an overwhelming inclination towards secularity of state affairs as an effective remedy to a large number of internal problems.

Turkmenistan and Uzbekistan are both former republics of the Soviet Union. The Republic of Turkmenistan is located in Central Asia east of the Caspian Sea, bordering Uzbekistan, Kazakhstan, Iran, and Afghanistan. Turkmenistan has an area of approximately 188,500 square miles and its capital is Ashkhabad. Uzbekistan is the main Muslim cultural center. The republic gained its independence in 1991. It is bordered on the north and northwest by Kazakhstan, on the east and southeast by Kyrgyzstan and Tajikistan, on the southwest by Turkmenistan, and on the south by Afghanistan. These republics' reactions to the Taliban's progress have been divergent. For instance the Taliban showed a great deal of reluctance when Uzbekistan closed the port of Hairatan even before the capture of Mazar-e-Sharif. They were also annoyed because of the cessation of the trade flux from Mazar and Shiberghan as a result of the closure. When Turkmenistan, on the other hand, allowed trade to be carried out through Turkmenistan's border which is near Andkhoui (which borders the provinces of Faryab and Jowzjan), the Taliban considered that a grace from Allah. It must be borne in mind with some certainty that the Taliban's final prevalence led some countries to commence their investment in Afghanistan.

In an overall view, it is worth mentioning that with all of the ups and downs in their commercial evaluation of the future of

Afghanistan, these northern neighbouring republics agree on the point that they do not wish to witness the spread of an Islam represented by the Taliban in their territories. Hence their attitudes towards Afghanistan would be ultimately determined by this.

8

Bin Laden

Osama bin Laden was named by US officials as a prime suspect in two deadly bombings in Saudi Arabia, when some 24 American military personnel and two Indians were killed in the blasts in Riyadh and at a barrack in the eastern city of al-Khobar.

Bin Laden denied involvement in the bombings but said they were warnings that the United States should withdraw its forces from Saudi Arabia. Four Saudis who said in confessions on Saudi television that they were influenced by Bin Laden and other Saudi dissidents were beheaded for the Riyadh bombing.

Bin Laden called for a jihad, or holy war, "against the Americans who are occupying the land of the two shrines", Saudi Arabia. He referred to the American forces in the Gulf as a "crusader" army. Bin Laden had earlier said: "I believe that sooner or later the Americans will leave Saudi Arabia and that the war declared by America against the Saudi people means war against all Muslims everywhere."

He was quoted saying "Resistance against America will spread in many, many places in Muslim countries. Our trusted leaders, the *ulema* (religious scholars), have given us a *fatwa* (Islamic edict) that we must drive out the Americans. The solution to this crisis is the withdrawal of American troops...their military presence is an insult for the Saudi people." The US State Department recently called Bin Laden "one of the most significant sponsors of Islamic extremist activities in the world today."

Bin Laden's Life

Osama bin Mohammad bin Laden was born in the city of Riyadh 1957. He was raised in Medina and received his education in the schools of Jedda, then studied management and economics in King Abdul Aziz University in Jedda. Bin Laden is married and has children. He began his interaction with Islamic groups in 1973 and continued concentrating on Islamic concerns in modern times until the commencement of jihad in Afghanistan. He is reported to have maintained links, in the beginning of the eighties, with the Mujahideen against the Communist party in South Yemen. His contribution to Afghan Mujahideen until the downfall of the Communist party is considered to be enormous.

He established alongside Sheikh Dr Abdullah Azzam the office for Mujahideen services in Peshawar, founding again in partnership with Sheikh Azzam the Sidda camp for the training of Arab Mujahideen who came for jihad in Afghanistan. His first visit to assist the Afghan Mujahideen started a few days after the Russian invasion of Afghanistan in 1979. He laid the foundation of "Ma`sadat Al-Ansar" which was a base for Arab Mujahideen in Afghanistan. In 1986 he participated in the battles of Jalalabad with the Arab Mujahideen which was one of the best known battles for the extensive involvement of Arabs.

He left Saudi Arabia in 1991, refusing to return later despite calls from the Saudi government. As a result Saudis reportedly withdrew his citizenship, cancelled his passport, froze his assets, and launched a media campaign against him.

He currently resides in Afghanistan, and has given a call to the Muslims throughout the world to declare a jihad against the Judao–Christian alliance which is occupying Islamic sacred land in Palestine and the Arabian Peninsula.

His Outlook

Bin Laden views the conflict in the light of "Muslim believers who are confronted with disbelievers (*Kuffar*, heathen). In his view, the term, "disbelievers" encompasses the "pragmatic" Arab regimes (including the government of his own homeland, Saudi Arabia), and the United States, which he sees as taking over the Muslim holy sites of Mecca and Medina, and assisting the Jews in their conquest of Palestine.

Bin Laden's views are simple and more or less shared by the rest of Sunni and even Shi'te revivalists groups. This world view not only encourages the use of military and physical force but sanctifies this by religious edict. For Bin Laden, political gains through force have the standing of a religious injunction. He sees the "jihad" as necessary to raise the Muslim world above the world of the disbelievers, and argues that military action is justified by the degraded moral standards of his enemies, the Christians and the Jews. The United States, he maintains, is responsible for the most reprehensible acts of world terrorism, such as the bombing of Hiroshima and Nagasaki, and carpet bombing of Iraq. While the Zionists, whom he refers to in terms reminiscent of the writers of "the Protocols of the Elders of Zion", are held responsible for the massacres of Dir Yassin, Sabra and Shatila in Palestine and Lebanon.

In order to perform his religious "duties", Bin Laden founded the "International Islamic Front for jihad against the Jews and the Crusaders." This organisation published a *"fatwa"* (religious ruling) proclaiming the "jihad against disbelievers who conquer Muslim lands" a duty incumbent upon all believing Muslims.

Bin Laden's name has come up in connection with a number of attacks around the world, among them the attacks in Riyadh (November 95) and Dhahran (June 96), that left a number people dead, including Americans. He is also implicated in the attacks on a Yeminite hotel (December 92) that injured several tourists; the assassination attempt on Egyptian president Mubarak in Ethiopia (June 95); the World Trade Centre bombing (February 93) that killed 3 and injured hundreds; and the Somali attack on American forces that left hundreds wounded.

Although Bin Laden denies his involvement, he however does not hide his admiration for those who carried out the attacks. Bin Laden praised in particular the perpetrators of the Riyadh bombing, referring to the four men who were executed by the Saudis as "*shahids*", or martyrs, who paved the way for other true believers.

Bin Laden plays an important role in supporting and enlarging the pool of Islamic fighters known as the "Afghan Veterans." Today a large number of militants in Afghanistan owe allegiance to him. At the same time he maintains extensive ties with a number of international Islamic organisations in Egypt, India, the Philippines, and elsewhere. These organisations reportedly enjoy the use of Bin Laden's funding, his training camps, and possibly even his many companies around the world. Bin Laden's opponents believe these companies are invaluable to Islamic activists in furnishing logistic and communication support, as well as providing cover. Bin Laden's adversaries hold that the principal danger presented by Bin Laden is the combination of tremendous financial resources coupled with an extremist ideology backed, in his view, by heavenly decree; an ideology which advocates the wholesale demolition of its perceived enemies, whether soldiers or civilians, children or adults. To them, the alliance of such an individual with a group of trained and experienced fighters, steeped in Islamic indoctrination, is potentially deadly. All the more so when the fighters are veterans of a long, and for their part, victorious war for the sake of religion. Such a combination is a recipe for acts of political violence and mass destruction. One cannot rule out the possibility of an organisation espousing such a doctrine employing non-conventional methods. In the estimation of many security analysts, this combination of wealth and extremism gives the Afghan Veterans Association a place among the most dangerous organisations threatening the Western powers and their allies in the Islamic world.

Bin Laden and the *Fatwa* against the US

The following words are reported to have been made available to world media as a religious ruling issued by
• Shaykh Osamah Bin-Muhammad Bin-Laden
• Ayman al-Zawahiri, Amir of the Jihad Group in Egypt
• Yasir Rifa'i Ahmad Taha, a leader of the (Egyptian) Islamic Group

- Shaykh Mir Hamzah, secretary of the Jamiat-ul-Ulema-e-Pakistan
- Fazlul Rahman, Amir of the Jihad Movement in Bangladesh

A close contemplation on ideas incorporated in this *fatwa* is of guidance to Bin Laden's world view.

Prolegomenon to the main text of the *Fatwa*:
"Praise be to Allah, who revealed the Book, controls the clouds, defeats factionalism, and says in His Book 'But when the forbidden months are past, then fight and slay the pagans wherever ye find them, seize them, beleaguer them, and lie in wait for them in every stratagem (of war)'; and peace be upon our Prophet, Muhammad Bin-'Abdallah, who said I have been sent with the sword between my hands to ensure that no one but Allah is worshipped, Allah who put my livelihood under the shadow of my spear and who inflicts humiliation and scorn on those who disobey my orders. The Arabian Peninsula has never, since Allah made it flat, created its desert, and encircled it with seas, been stormed by any forces like the crusader armies spreading in it like locusts, eating its riches and wiping out its plantations. All this is happening at a time in which nations are attacking Muslims like people fighting over a plate of food. In the light of the grave situation and the lack of support, we and you are obliged to discuss current events, and we should all agree on how to settle the matter.

No one argues today about three facts that are known to everyone; we will list them, in order to remind everyone:
First, for over seven years the United States has been occupying the lands of Islam in the holiest of places, the Arabian Peninsula, plundering its riches, dictating to its rulers, humiliating its people, terrorising its neighbours, and turning its bases in the Peninsula into a spearhead through which to fight the neighbouring Muslim peoples.

If some people have in the past argued about the fact of the occupation, all the people of the Peninsula have now acknowledged it.

The best proof of this is the Americans' continuing aggression against the Iraqi people using the Peninsula as a staging post, even though all its rulers are against their territories being used to that end, but they are helpless.

Second, despite the great devastation inflicted on the Iraqi people by the Crusader-Zionist alliance, and despite the huge number of those killed, which has exceeded 1 million... despite all this, the Americans are once again trying to repeat the horrific massacres, as though they are not content with the protracted blockade imposed after the ferocious war or the fragmentation and devastation. So here they come to annihilate what is left of this people and to humiliate their Muslim neighbours.

Third, if the American aims behind these wars are religious and economic, the aim is also to serve the Jews' petty state and divert attention from its occupation of Jerusalem and murder of Muslims there.

The best proof of this is their eagerness to destroy Iraq, the strongest neighbouring Arab state, and their endeavour to fragment all the states of the region such as Iraq, Saudi Arabia, Egypt, and Sudan into paper states through their disunity and weakness to guarantee Israel's survival and the continuation of the brutal crusade occupation of the Peninsula.

All these crimes and sins committed by the Americans are a clear declaration of war on Allah, His Messenger, and Muslims. And the *ulema* have throughout Islamic history unanimously agreed that jihad is an individual duty if the enemy destroys Muslim countries. This was revealed by Imam ibn-Qadamah in "*Al-Mughni*," Imam al-Kisa'i in "*Al-Bada'i*," Al-Qurtubi in his interpretation, and the Shaykh of al-Islam in his books, where he said "As for the fighting to repulse (an enemy), it is aimed at defending sanctity and religion, and it is a duty as agreed (by the *ulema*). Nothing is more sacred than belief in repulsing an enemy who is attacking religion and life."

Main Text of the *Fatwa*:
"On that basis, and in compliance with God's order, we issue the following *fatwa* to all Muslims:

The ruling to kill the Americans and their allies is an individual duty for every Muslim who can do it in any country in which it is possible to do it, in order to liberate the Al-Aqsa Mosque and the

Holy Mosque (Mecca) from their grip, and in order for their armies to move out of all the lands of Islam, defeated and unable to threaten any Muslim. This is in accordance with the words of Allah, "and fight the pagans all together as they fight you all together," and "fight them until there is no more tumult or oppression, and there prevail justice and faith in Allah."

This is in addition to the words of Almighty God "And why should ye not fight in the cause of God and of those who, being weak, are ill treated (and oppressed), women and children, whose cry is 'Our Lord, rescue us from this town, whose people are oppressors; and raise for us from thee one who will help!'"

We, with God's help, call on every Muslim who believes in Allah and wishes to be rewarded to comply with God's order to kill the Americans and plunder their money wherever and whenever they find it. We also call on Muslim *ulema*, leaders, youths, and soldiers to launch the raid on Satan's US troops and the devil's supporters allying with them, and to displace those who are behind them so that they may learn a lesson.

Almighty God said "O ye who believe, give your response to Allah and His Apostle, when He calleth you to that which will give you life. And know that Allah cometh between a man and his heart, and that it is He to whom ye shall all be gathered."

Almighty God also says "O ye who believe, what is the matter with you, that when ye are asked to go forth in the cause of Allah, ye cling so heavily to the earth! Do ye prefer the life of this world to the hereafter? But little is the comfort of this life, as compared with the hereafter."

American and Taliban Row over Bin Laden

In response to bombings in US embassies in Africa, the Clinton administration decided to target Bin Laden and his organisation. Areas of Afghanistan identified by US as Bin Laden's concentration of troops and equipments were bombarded.

The three training bases at Khost, Afghanistan were suspected by Americans of being used by a number of groups associated with the

Bin Laden network. The US announced that the bases provided refuge for terrorists and housed the infrastructure for their funding and international travel, and for training them in tactics and in the assembly and use of a wide variety of weapons. Several of these groups housed in these bases were declared by the US as foreign terrorist organisations who had conducted a variety of terrorist operations around the world. The American government indicated that it had reliable intelligence that the Bin Laden network had been actively seeking to acquire weapons of mass destruction, including chemical weapons, for use against United States interests. The US also attacked one facility in Sudan allegedly associated with chemical weapons and the Bin Laden network.

As a result of the American attacks on what the Taliban consider to be their territories twenty-six people were killed but Bin Laden was unhurt.

The Taliban furiously refused to hand over Bin Laden to the United States, saying even more Tomahawk cruise missiles would not persuade them to do so. However after a series of disputes and even threats by the US the Taliban came up with a waylaying idea. They specified a deadline before which the US was requested to hand over sufficient evidence in support of its demand for extradition of Bin Laden. This solution could spare the Taliban from accusations of co-operation with international terrorism as well as provide them with enough time to handle the Bin Laden dilemma.

By expiry of the deadline, on 20 November 1998, Bin Laden was declared a free man by the Taliban.

Afghanistan's chief justice, Noor Mohammed Saqib, said the United States had failed to provide any evidence and concluded "Without any evidence, Bin Laden is a man without sin...He is a free man."

However the US-Taliban dispute over Bin Laden is far from over. Despite assurances given by Amir Khan Mutaqqi, Taliban minister for information that Bin Laden is said not to engage in activities considered to be acts of international terrorism, the US offered a $5 million reward for the capture of Bin Laden, something the Taliban said was tantamount to encouraging terrorist activity inside their war-shattered country.

Bin Laden's future might be determined by various factors including the Taliban chances in coming to terms with the international community and their need to offer concessions towards the economic and political stability they are looking for.

9

A Word on the Taliban–UN Dilemma

The UN has not yet been in a position to offer the Taliban the seat of Afghanistan. This is the result of an awkward situation caused by the Taliban performance in regards to their tough stand on social policies as well as massacres allegedly committed by them. Another factor is that the UN still believes that the continuation of armed conflict in Afghanistan and the Taliban imposition of ethnic and religious policies on their opponents are a recipe for instability and a violation of human rights. The Taliban, though practically ready to enter any kind of talks, have, in turn, made it clear at least locally that the UN is theologically representing notions alien to Islamic sociology.

In an official statement Mufti Rasheed Ahmad Sahib from Darul Ifta-e-Wal Irshad (the Issuing House of *Fatwa* and Guidance) Karachi, said:

"It is compulsory and a debt upon the Muslims to provide moral, political, military and financial support to the heroes of Islam the Taliban who are free from the destructive yoke of the World Bank, IMF, UN and others. Remember! Only the Taliban can help the Islamic World out of their internal and external crisis. Anti-Islam forces are bending over backwards to economically crush this new born pure Islamic state, before it becomes a world economic power."

Remarks made by Mulla Muhammad Rabbani head of the Interim Council addressing a large number of *ulema* could be an indication of the image presented by the Taliban of the UN to their audience inside Afghanistan. These remarks which are in *Dharb-i-Mumin* are as follows:

Mulla Rabbani criticized America, the UN and all other western non-Islamic countries saying that until yesterday they had been making tall claims of finding a peaceful solution to the Afghan problem of establishing complete peace in the continent, but today, because of the implementation of Sharee'ah, they had turned against Afghanistan. Today, the Islamic Emirate is the greatest obstacle in the way of the *Kufriah* (heathen) states, he said. Their opposition is, ironically, proof that we are in the right. Referring to the Jews as the sworn enemies of Islam, Mulla Rabbani condemned the former president Burhanuddin Rabbani for seeking the help of Israel against the Taliban. Rabbani has invited upon himself the wrath of Allah Ta'ala, he denounced. About Iran he said that its intervention and opposition had greatly increased after the Taliban's capture of Herat, but that its military support to the anti-Taliban factions had come to nothing. Now, to hide evidence of its massive arms supply it was crying foul over the killings of its diplomats. Mulla Muhammad Rabbani said that Iran should not attack Afghanistan, for if it did so it will suffer for it. Scars of its war with Iraq are still fresh, so it should not make the same mistake again. "We are sure that Iran cannot bear the burden of another long, terrible war," he said. "The recent killings of innocent Afghan refugees in Iran is a slur upon the names of UN and Iran itself," he added.

However, it would be unwise to perceive Rabbani's words as the final attitude of the Taliban towards the United Nations. Contacts between the UN envoys as well as its various representatives with the Taliban are indicative of the fact that the movement is ready to show a great deal of flexibility on issues of a temporary nature. The dilemma will remain if the UN and other countries continue pressing their demands concerning improvements in the human rights situation in Afghanistan or the distribution of power between the Taliban and other groups who are not representative of political or military strengths. In the latter case, the Taliban would not be in a position to offer required concessions since this would lead to vast internal disarray and an ultimately precarious situation for the movement.

The UN, in turn, are under pressures from various groups and countries not to assist the Taliban with their claims. Calls for an end to Taliban policies which prohibit women from seeking employment and education have come from many Afghan civil rights groups. These include the Advisory Group on Gender Issues in Afghanistan, made up of Afghan men and women working for UN agencies and NGOs handling aid programs in the country. There are groups who persistently call on the UN and member states to safeguard basic human rights in Afghanistan and urge them to take "careful account" of the Taliban's human rights record when considering their request for recognition or assistance for reconstruction in Afghanistan. Afghan women's rights groups, notably the Revolutionary Association of the Women of Afghanistan and the Afghan Women's Council based in Peshawar, Pakistan, have made similar appeals to the international community to protect women's human rights in Afghanistan.

Despite these calls, the UN must bear in mind that Afghanistan is actually and in real terms ruled by the Taliban and that this is a fact which must not be ignored or even underestimated. The division of opinions over consideration of the Taliban administration as the Afghanistan government is fact. However, an unexpected sequence of events overshadows the whole procedure of thinking and at times shatters the plans for taking further steps towards the Taliban. In November 1998, an Afghan employee of the United Nations was reported to have been shot and killed by Taliban troops when they overran central Bamiyan in August. Sayed Essa, a guard at the WFP warehouse, was apparently killed while fleeing into the mountains to avoid advancing Taliban forces, the statement said. The WFP is the United Nations' front-line agency in the fight against hunger and has operations in 76 countries around the world.

The United Nations on Tuesday 20 October 1998 refused to recognize the Taliban as Afghanistan's legitimate government for the third time in as many years and kept the UN seat with the representative of ousted President Burhanuddin Rabbani. As it did in each of the past two years, the UN credentials committee deferred a decision on the two sets of credentials it received from representatives of the Taliban and Rabbani, meaning the seat will stay with Rabbani's envoy for another year.

The Taliban's envoy in New York, Abdul Hakeem Mujahid, had contacted the countries on the committee and lobbied for the Taliban cause. The Taliban presented an account of their position in a 10-page document that lists the reasons why the Taliban should be recognized as the true government of Afghanistan and explaining their position on human rights, women's rights, drug proliferation and tensions with Iran and other neighboring countries.

They said :

"The time has come to give Afghanistan what the world owes it, a chance to build on what works well for Afghans."

The Taliban concluded:

"Recognition of the Islamic Emirates of Afghanistan has no ill consequences to any nation and will be a great and good step for the fiercely independent people of Afghanistan."

Conclusion

Years of fervent strife in replacing the communist regime in Afghanistan with a purely Islamic government - a government that could be approved by the majority of Afghans - did not come to a happy ending. No sooner than acquiring political power, the Muslim warriors submerged themselves in a ferocious civil war. In the midst of this conflict there emerged a new group of jihad called the Taliban. The latter waged war against all other Mujahideen claiming that the latter had violated their allegiance to Islam by acknowledging the liberal and modern maxims of political and social life and by engaging in an internal bloodshed that humiliated Islam and the Islamic land of Afghanistan. This group unexpectedly and mysteriously, or miraculously as they put it, subdued all other major parties and groups and dominated the main political arena. Their advance to the most strategic position was complete once they triumphantly conquered the major strongholds of the Mujahideen and Kabul in particular. In the light of circumstantial and material evidence, the group was supported by forces outside Afghanistan. These forces were apparently willing to put an end to disruptive and agitating civil war in Afghanistan. The Taliban received moral and material aid from their fellow religionists in Pakistan. The disciplined organisation, as well as the quality and quantity of arsenal utilised by the Taliban, suggest that their campaign had the blessing of well-founded and expertly organised supporters. Their administration was almost immediately recognised by Pakistan, Saudi Arabia and the Emirates. The Taliban first took the world by surprise through their vigorous and victorious appearance on battlefronts and then through their tenacious attachment to their own brand of fundamentalist Islam that generated dramatic results. These included the exclusion of women from education and persecution of individuals under various charges of defiance. Yet the Taliban are still far from ultimate success. This is a fact that manifests itself at various levels.

1. The Taliban could not complete the annihilation of the Mujahideen Islamic government that is currently represented by the most gifted military commander, Ahmad Shah Masoud. The latter, being aided by the Taliban's many powerful opponents, poses a permanent threat to the stability of Taliban control of the land. Furthermore, the physical existence of a rather massive military defiance against the Taliban serves as an extra justification for keeping them out of the UN and subsequent forms of international recognition. Interacting with other anti-Taliban elements including the Iranian mobilised battalions and military and financial aid flooded on Ahmad from various resources, the Taliban have been persuaded that military action might not be the final solution to all their problems and that they may consider setbacks in their radical policies sooner or later.

2. In respect of their theological principles, the Taliban gradually learned how to bring together politics with religious fanatical attitudes. Their reconciliatory positions towards the Iranian threat of invasion and their offer of co-operation denote they clearly realise that their safe and immune grip on power comes before all other considerations. The subsequent negotiations with Iran persuaded both sides that they can do business with each other. However, flexibility in attitudes might just be possible as far as foreign policy is concerned and a firm reliance on radical fanaticism inside the country is still the wisest option.

3. As for political organisation, there is still a need to evolve a system compatible with a caliphate-based form of administration. However, the latest structuring and restructuring of the organisational realm of politics signify the massive impact of modern norms of governmental organisation on the Taliban's administration.

4. In respect of economy, the Taliban's choices are extremely limited. Lacking an economic agenda, they have either to take the risk of extemporaneous planning that could lead to disastrous situations or abide by international financing and economic prescriptions. As far as foreign investments are concerned, the Taliban have shown a great deal of interest and appetite. They are

duly prepared to take steps necessary to ensure the security of foreign capital invested in various projects of interest. Yet, with regards to legalities essential to win the confidence of foreign investors and measures needed to pave for these investments such as international recognition, the Taliban still have a long way to go.

5. The self-promoting policy of the Taliban, or what might be called "the export of their brand of Islam", has proven to be exceedingly unpopular with regional and international governments. This policy has aroused antipathy towards the Taliban in neighbouring countries with Muslim populations. The movement may have realised by now that stirring up internal difficulties in Pakistan, coupled with economy and security-motivated proximity with their foreign and Afghan opponents, could turn the balance of power against them. However, as previously mentioned, the Taliban government has clearly demonstrated its essential craving for survival and this can lead them to all sorts of unforeseen alliances.

6. With regards human rights and gender issues, a drastic shift in the Taliban policies seems to be out of scope for the time being. However, the desire for consolidation of political and economic control that may only come about via the betterment of the Taliban's international image could force them to consider improvements in that direction.

Further Reading

A History of Afghanistan, trans: Vitaly Baskakov, Firebird Publishings

Adventures in Afghanistan, Louis Palmer, Octagon Press

Afghan Alternatives: Issues, Options and Policies, ed. Ralph H. Magnus, Transaction Pub

Afghan Nomads in Transition: A Century of Change Among the Zala Khan Khel (The Carlsberg Foundation's Nomad Research Project), Ida Nicolaisen, Gorm Pedersen, Thames & Hudson

Afghan Resistance: The Politics of Survival, ed. Grant M. Farr and John G. Merriam, Westview Press

Afghan Wars, 1839-1992: What Britain Gave Up and the Soviet Union Lost, Edgar O'Balance, Brasseys Inc

Afghanistan (Country Guide Series Report from the Aacrao-Aid Project), Holly A. O'Neill, Amer Assn of Coll Registrars

Afghanistan (Cultures of the World), Sharifah Enayat, Marshal Cavendish Corp

Afghanistan (Enchantment of the World), Leila Merrell Foster, Childrens Press

Afghanistan: Agony of a Nation, Sandy Gall, Bodley Head

Afghanistan: Fighting for Freedom (Discovering Our Heritage), Mir T. Ansary, Dillon Press

Afghanistan: Paradise Lost, Roland Michaud, Rizzoli Intl. Pubns.

Afghanistan: The Soviet Invasion and the Afghan Response, 1979-1982, M. Hasan Kakar, University of California Press

Afghanistan: The Soviet Invasion in Perspective (Publication 321), Anthony Arnold, Hoover Inst Press

Afghanistan and the Soviet Union, Henry S. Bradsher, Duke University Press

Afghanistan Crises, Tahir Amin, Holy Koran Publishing House

Afghanistan Dar Panj Qarn Akheer (in Dari) (Afghanistan in the Past Five Centuries), Mir M. Sediq Farhang, Sanai Publishing

Afghanistan du communisme au Fondamentalisme, Sylvie Gélinas, L. Harmattan, Paris

Afghanistan in Crisis, K. P. Misra, Stosius Inc/Advent Books Division

Afghanistan Mongolia and USSR, Ram Rahul, Vikas Publishing House

Afghanistan of the Afghans, Shah Sirdar Ikbal Ali, Shah Sirdar Ikbal Ali

Afghanistan, Louis Dupree, Princeton University Press

Afghanistan, the Soviet Union's Last War, Mark Galeotti, Frank Cass & Co

Afghanistan: A Profile, Ralph H. Magnus, Westview Press

Afghanistan: Between the Past and the Future, Lev Nikolayev, Progress Publishers

Afghanistan: Highway of Conquest, Arnold Fletcher, Cornell University Press
Afghanistan: The Great Game Revisited, ed. Rosanne Klass, Freedom House
Afghanistan's Two-Party Communism: Parcham and Khalq, Anthony Arnold, Hoover Inst Press
Among the Afghans (Central Asia Book Series), Arthur Bonner, Duke University Press
Archaeology of Afghanistan: From Earliest Times to the Timurid Period, F. R. Allchin, N. Hammond (Editor), Academic Press
Between Two Giants: Political History of Afghanistan in the 19th century, Sayed Qaseem Reshtia, Afghan Jehad Works Translation Centre, 1990
Bridgehead Afghanistan, Wilhelm Dietl, South Asia Books
British and American Responses to the Soviet Invasion of Afghanistan, Gabriella Grasselli, Dartmouth Pub. Co.
Buzkashi: Game and Power in Afghanistan, G. Whitney Azoy, University of Pennsylvania Press
Caravans to Tartary, Sabrina Michaud, Roland Michaud, Thames & Hudson
Caught in the Crossfire, Jan Goodwin, E. P. Dutton
Cultural Policy in Afghanistan, Shafie Rahel, UNESCO Press
Danziger's Adventures; from Miami to Kabul, Nick Danziger, HarperCollins
Danziger's Travels, Nick Danziger, Flamingo / HarperCollins
Dictionary of Afghan Wars, Revolutions, and Insurgencies (Historical Dictionaries of Wars, Revolution, and Civil Unrest, No. 1), Ludwig W. Adamec, Scarecrow Press
Disposable People? The Plight of Refugees, Judy Mayotte, Orbis Books
Fundamentalism Reborn? Afghanistan and the Taliban, ed. William Maley, C. Hurst & Co. Publishers
Gemstones of Afghanistan, Bonita Chamberlin Bowersox, Bonita E. Chamberlin, Gary W. Bowersox, Mountain Press
Gemstones of Afghanistan, Gary W. Bowersox, Geoscience Press
Gorbachev's Afghan Gambit (National Security Paper. 9), Theodore L. Eliot, Inst. Foreign Policy Analysis
Guerrilla Strategies: An Historical Anthology from the Long March to Afghanistan, Gerard Chaliand, University of California Press
Hazaras of Afghanistan, S. Mousavi, St. Martin's Press
Heroes of the Age: Moral Fault Lines on the Afghan Frontier (Comparative Studies on Muslim Societies No. 21), David B. Edwards, Univ of California Press
Historical Dictionary of Afghanistan, Ludwig W. Adamec, Scarecrow Press
Holy Blood: An Inside View of the Afghan War, Paul Overby, Praeger Pub Text
Holy War, Unholy Victory: Eyewitness to the CIA's Secret War in Afghanistan, Kurt Lohbeck, Regnery Publishing, Inc.
Inside the Soviet Army in Afghanistan, Alex Alexiev, Rand Corp
Islam and Politics in Afghanistan, Asta Olesen, Curzon Press
Islamic Fundamentalism in Afghanistan? Its Character and Prospects, Graham E. Fuller, Rand Corp.

Life of the Amir Dost Mohammed Khan of Kabul, Mohan Lal, Oxford University Press

My Life—From Brigand to King, Amir Habibullah Khan, Octagon Press

Oral Narrative in Afghanistan: The Individual in Tradition, Margaret Ann Mills, Garland Pub

Out of Afghanistan: The Inside Story of the Soviet Withdrawal, Diego Cordovez and Selig S. Harrison, Oxford University Press

Permian Stratigraphy and Fusulinida of Afghanistan With Their Paleogeographic and Paleotectonic Implications, E. Ia Leven, Calvin H. Stevens, Donald L. Baars, Geological Society of America

Politics of Women and Development in Afghanistan, Hafizullah Emadi, Paragon House

Prigioniero in Afghanistan (Italian - Prisoner in Afghanistan), Fausto Biloslavo, Sugar Co

Reform and Rebellion in Afghanistan, 1919-1929: King Amanullah's Failure to *Modernize a Tribal Society*, Leon B. Poullada, Cornell University Press

Rhetorics and Politics in Afghan Traditional Storytelling, Margaret A. Mills, University of Pennsylvania Press

Russian Roulette: Afghanistan Through Russian Eyes, Gennady Bocharov. Trans. Alyona Kojevnikov, A Cornelia and Michael Bessie Book/ HarperCollins

Searching for Saleem: An Afghan Woman's Odyssey, Farooka Gauhari, University of Nebraska Press

Shadow Over Afghanistan, Fazel Rahman Fazel, Western Book/Journal Press

Soldiers of God: With the Mujahideen in Afghanistan, Robert D. Kaplan, Houghton Mifflin Company

Soviet-American Relations with Pakistan, Iran, and Afghanistan, Hafeez Malik, St. Martin's Press

State, Revolution, and Superpowers in Afghanistan, Hafizullah Emadi, Praeger Pub

Stumbling Bear: Soviet Military Performance in Afghanistan, Scott R. McMichael, Brasseys Inc

The 'Ancient Supremacy': Bukhara, Afghanistan and the Battle for Balkh, 1731-1901 (Islamic History and Civilization, No. 15), Jonathan L. Lee, E J Brill

The Central Asian Arabs of Afghanistan: Pastoral Nomadism in Transition, Thomas J. Barfield, University of Texas Press

The Constitutional Decade (Dari), Sabah Kushkaki, Cultural Council of Afghanistan Resistance

The Cultural Basis of Afghan Nationalism, Editors: Ewan W. Anderson and Nancy Hatch Dupree, Printer Publishers

The Fall of Afghanistan: An Insider's Account, Abdul Samad Ghaus, Brasseys Inc

The Fateful Pebble: Afghanistan's Role in the Fall of the Soviet Empire, Anthony Arnold, Presidio Press

The Hazaras, Hassan Poladi, Mughal Publishing co

The Hidden War: A Russian Journalist's Account of the Soviet War in Afghanistan, Artyom Borovik, Atlantic Monthly Press

The History of the Saffarids of Sistan and the Maliks of Nimruz (247/861 to 949/ 1542-3), Clifford Edmund Bosworth, Mazda Pub

The Later Ghaznavids: Splendour and Decay: The Dynasty in Afghanistan and Northern India, 1040-1186, Clifford Edmund Bosworth, Mazda Publications

The light garden of the angel king: journeys in Afghanistan, Peter Levi, Collins

The Pathans: 500 BC-AD 1957, Olaf Caroe, Oxford University Press

The Politics of Afghanistan, Richard S. Newell, Cornell University Press

The Politics of Social Transformation in Afghanistan, Iran, and Pakistan (Contemporary Issues in the Middle East), ed. Ali Banuazizi, Myron Weiner, Syracuse University Press

The Red Army on Pakistan's Border: Policy Implications for the United States (Foreign Policy Report), ed. Theodore L. Eliot, Brasseys Inc

The Road to Oxiana, Robert Byron, Oxford Univ Press

The Soviet Withdrawal from Afghanistan, William Maley (Editor), Amin Saikal, Cambridge University Press

The Taliban, Peter Marsden, Oxford Univ Press

The Tragedy of Afghanistan: A First-Hand Account, Raja Anwar, Fred Halliday, Khalid Hasan (Translator), Verso Books

Untying of the Afghan Knot: Negotiating Soviet Withdrawal, Riaz M. Khan, Duke University Press

Valley of the Giant Buddhas, Morag Murray Abdullah, Octagon Press

War Without Winners: Afghanistan's Uncertain Transition After the Cold War, Rasul Bakhsh Rais, Oxford University Press

Index